# Praise for
# *What Do You Really Want?*

"Cayla's *What Do You* Really *Want?* is a game changer! Immerse yourself in her profound insights and let her lead you beyond fear, straight to your dreams. This isn't just a book; it's a call to action, a blueprint for discovering your true desires and chasing them without hesitation. Find your unstoppable essence within its pages. A must-read!"

— JEN GOTTLIEB, AUTHOR OF *BE SEEN* AND COFOUNDER OF SUPER CONNECTOR MEDIA

"*What Do You* Really *Want?* is a life-altering book for those ready to elevate their existence. Cayla unveils innovative methods to break free from self-imposed obstacles and helps you shift your mindset to ditch the good and go for the great. With this insight, no goal is too audacious or unattainable. If you're like me and want to make the highest possible return on your investment, I highly recommend that you invest in yourself by reading this book! It is a must-read for everyone striving to overcome their inner barriers and wanting to change their lives."

— VEENA JETTI, FOUNDER OF VIVE FUNDS AND MOTIVATIONAL SPEAKER

"Cayla Craft's new book is so timely. In a world that is full of uncertainties and life interruptions, she shows us how to realign with our childhood innocence. Cayla is known for getting results in everything she does. Every chapter in this book will bring you closer to the person you've been created to be."

— TIM STOREY, BESTSELLING AUTHOR, MOTIVATIONAL SPEAKER, AND PASTOR

"Remember the *audacity* of childhood dreams? Before the world drowned out your inner voice and molded your wants based on others' expectations and standards? Cayla has crafted more than just a book; it's a guide leading you back to that unfiltered, raw version of yourself. *What Do You Really Want?* doesn't merely ask—it shouts, challenges, and charts the way forward. If self-doubt has ever clipped your wings, let this book be the wind beneath them. It's not just about reading; it's about awakening. Every woman needs this book to unleash her truest dreams and desires."

— AKEMI SUE FISHER, AMAZON QUEEN, THOUGHT LEADER, BUSINESS STRATEGIST, AND MONEY MENTOR

"If you struggle with self-sabotage and negative patterns that prevent you from living your most purposeful life, this book is for you. My friend Cayla Craft's proven techniques will help you step into the life God has for you!"
—B. SIMONE, COMEDIAN AND ENTREPRENEUR

# What Do You Really Want?

# What Do You Really Want?

## 7 Questions That Can Unlock the Answers to a Life Full of Abundance, Meaning, and Connection

## Cayla Craft

NELSON
BOOKS

An Imprint of Thomas Nelson

### Library of Congress Cataloging-in-Publication Data

Names: Craft, Cayla, 1987- author.
Title: What do you really want? : 7 questions that can unlock the answers to a life full of abundance, meaning, and connection / Cayla Craft.
Description: Nashville : Thomas Nelson, 2024. | Includes bibliographical references. | Summary: "Successful entrepreneur and life coach Cayla Craft reveals to readers the seven questions that can unlock a new paradigm for dreaming, envisioning, and activating the life story they want to live"-- Provided by publisher.
Identifiers: LCCN 2023040467 (print) | LCCN 2023040468 (ebook) | ISBN 9781400245819 (hardcover) | ISBN 9781400245833 (ebook)
Subjects: LCSH: Self-actualization (Psychology) | Self-realization.
Classification: LCC BF637.S4 C7238 2024 (print) | LCC BF637.S4 (ebook) | DDC 158.1--dc23/eng/20231127
LC record available at https://lccn.loc.gov/2023040467
LC ebook record available at https://lccn.loc.gov/2023040468

*Printed in the United States of America*

23 24 25 26 27 LBC 5 4 3 2 1

*To all my clients who went through this coaching process
and were brave enough to go after their dreams.*

*To my family, who inspires me every
day to go big or go home.*

*To everyone who reads this book, I am proud of you.*

# Contents

# CONTENTS

# Foreword

CAYLA AND I HAVE BEEN FRIENDS FOR A LONG time. When we met at a business event, I was immediately drawn to her like a magnet because of her bold, confident energy and demeanor. Like me, she's passionate about family, personal growth, and creative entrepreneurship. We've both spent a lot of time in the fitness space, for better or worse. What captivated me, though, was her personal story.

Cayla is a disruptor. When I see a woman out in the world breaking the patterns of where she came from while simultaneously reaching back and taking everyone around her with her, I know that's the type of woman I will fight to have in my circle. When you have women like Cayla in your life, you can't fail. She won't let you. She's a constant reminder of what's possible, no matter what system of beliefs you came from.

Cayla knew at a young age that she was meant for more. She felt a burning desire to help people. Even though the odds were stacked against her success, she worked hard and overcame a lot to become an ER nurse. But she wasn't satisfied—it wasn't what she *really* wanted. So as a young mom, she became an entrepreneur. That's when she got her first life-changing taste of success. She created a network of more than sixty thousand people in the health and wellness space and discovered she has a gift for helping others succeed. So she took charge of her life's narrative and began crafting the life of her dreams, coaching women to go after their own dreams and unapologetically achieve big.

Now she's living her best life—a life of abundance, meaning, and connection—because she discovered what she *really* wanted and boldly stepped out to make it happen. I love watching this woman raise her children so consciously, with her whole heart helping to guide and extract their greatness, while also coaching the next wave of changemakers in the same way. Everything she does is done at a level of excellence because Cayla won't settle . . . and we shouldn't either.

A self-made millionaire many times over, Cayla has coached countless entrepreneurial women to greater insight and confidence, helping them grow their businesses to seven figures and beyond. She draws on her own personal experience, equipping them with the tools and resources to shamelessly pursue their ambitions and life goals.

The only problem is that there's only one Cayla—and so many women need what she has to offer.

That's why I'm thrilled Cayla has written *What Do You Really Want?* In this book she coaches you to coach yourself the way she's coached so many other women to extraordinary growth and success.

Coaching can work wonders. I know this from personal experience. It's an intimate experience, custom made for you. The best coach will ask questions that lead to answers only you can provide. Cayla's the best coach. Her questions are top shelf. If you want to coach yourself to unprecedented success, this is the book for you. When you practice her Take 7 approach, you'll see amazing things start to happen in your life. You'll figure out what you *really* want and go for it. That's going to be positively life-changing. You'll be happier for it. And the world will be a better place when you realize your dreams.

Lori Harder
host of the *Earn Your Happy*
podcast, author, entrepreneur,
and founder of GLOCI

# Introduction

## *The Right Questions*

I'M SO GLAD YOU PICKED UP THIS BOOK. WE HAVE a lot in common, you and I! We make things happen. We dream big and work hard to achieve goals. We love our families.

See? We're a lot alike.

But you're not me. You've got your own angles, edges, facets, and shapes. Certain things make you happy. Others make you sad. Your life experiences—the good, the bad, and the ugly—shaped you to be exactly who you are.

I love helping women like you realize their fullest potential, make their dreams come true, and do it their way with their own flair. I'm in my zone helping them broaden their horizons, gain clarity and strategy, and live their best life by stepping into their

Your life

experiences—the

good, the bad, and

the ugly—shaped

you to be exactly

who you are.

calling. I've helped tens of thousands of women find and pursue their passions.

As I've coached these amazing women, I've learned that the very things that make us each so special and unique—our emotions and experiences—can easily get us stuck. It's not a lack of motivation or power. It's a lack of *clarity*.

Are you feeling stuck? Maybe you've plateaued or gotten discouraged because you haven't hit some past goals or dreams you've had for yourself. Or maybe you've thought, *I should be happy. Why aren't I happy?*

Listen, I've been there.

Paying attention to what we feel matters. We can gain terrific insights on how to move forward with even greater purpose and love. We can make astounding breakthroughs—if we ask and answer the right questions.

## The Right Questions

I get asked questions all the time. Because of my success, people ask me how I organize my business, how I track my momentum, what tools have helped me scale my entrepreneurial endeavors, what my skin routine looks like, and sometimes even what I eat for breakfast.

Those questions are valid. They're interesting and can be helpful. They might even lead to temporary change. But they won't bring significant, massive change. So let me ask you, *Are you asking the right questions?* Are you asking questions that will lead to a high-quality life? Or are you settling for inferior, low-quality questions?

*What's wrong with me?*

*Why can't I get ahead?*
*Why can't I catch a break?*

These are honest questions, for sure. Vulnerable questions. But not powerful ones. Those questions are self-deprecating and self-defeating. They won't clear the fog, get you unstuck, or move you closer to the life of your dreams. They aren't going to help you achieve your heart's desire.

What would your life look like if you started asking yourself excellent questions? I know that when I figured out the right questions to ask myself, my life changed. A lot. Asking the questions I came up with turned into a useful practice that changed my life and the lives of tens of thousands of women I've worked with. Once you learn this proven technique, you, too, will begin to identify your own blocks and overcome them.

The practice is simple and I call it Take 7. What, exactly, is Take 7? It's seven transformational questions:

1. **What's Not Working for Me in My Life?**

    This question helps you *voice* what's going on in your life that isn't in alignment with who you're made to be.

2. **When Did I First Start Accepting That?**

    This question prompts you to *get curious* about why you've been settling for less than you deserve.

3. **What Little Me Is Showing Up Right Now?**

    This question helps you *nurture* your inner child so that you can get out of your own way.

4. **What Is a Better Way of Looking at This?**

    This question helps *reframe* the story you're holding on to that no longer serves you.

5. **Where Is There Space for Gratitude in This?**

This question prompts *thanks* for the good, the bad, and the ugly.

6. **What Do I *Really* Want?**

This question helps you discover the *desire* of your heart.

7. **What Is the Best Next Step for Me?**

This question invites you to *act* in alignment with your vision.

As I've asked myself these questions at different times, I've seen how this practice has helped me develop a life that I love—one full of connection, purpose, and abundance. I've also seen profound and lasting changes in the lives of the women I've coached who have started asking themselves these seven questions.

And I want that to be your story too. I want you to use Take 7 to come to a greater understanding of what makes you tick. By using this practice and honestly answering these questions, you'll be able to clearly see what you *really* want, not just what you've been told you should want. You'll stop avoiding what needs to be confronted and let go of circumstances you can't change. You'll dream, plan, and create an actionable path for your life.

## When Should You Use Take 7?

The Take 7 practice is one that can be done at any time because these are questions your mind is primed to answer. You have these answers within you. There's no need to look outside

Take 7 has helped

me develop a life

that I love—one

full of connection,

purpose, and

abundance.

yourself. And that's why Take 7 is so empowering. These questions will help build your confidence and you'll realize how powerful you are.

You'll feel more equipped to go after what you really want. When you feel lost, on a detour, or frustrated, you'll gain clarity on what your feelings are telling you, be equipped to use that information, and then move closer to your goals. You'll know, bone deep, how profoundly and dramatically your stories shape you. And you'll start to write a new story.

However, there are specific times when Take 7 can be the most beneficial.

- **When you get stuck in your feelings.** Those times when you're overwhelmed, upset, confused, itchy for something new, feeling offended, defensive, or stuck on a problem.

- **When you need to make difficult decisions.** If you find yourself going back and forth and unable to make up your mind, it's likely that you need to take a few minutes and get in touch with what you really want.

- **When you want to make the good days even better.** When you're on track and everything's going well, you can use Take 7 to identify energy leaks or unprocessed emotions. You'll be able to get to where you want to go with ease by using Take 7.

- **When you are looking to free yourself** of whatever it is that's holding you back from living your best life. Take 7 will help you uncover blocks, unconscious thoughts, and limiting beliefs you've accepted for too long, plus illuminate the next step you need to take.

See, there's this fantasy—a modern fairy tale—that a single decision holds the key to your destiny. That's a lie. The truth is that a life is made up of *many* decisions. Your life is the sum of your decisions, which should be informed by your answers to these questions.

*You* get to decide what you want. You create the path to get what you want. You make a choice every single second of every single day. If you do the things that are aligned with your intention, you'll get there. And soon you'll see how little decisions—and big decisions—add up to a life you absolutely love.

The Take 7 practice is extremely powerful. Once you know how to use it, you can answer the questions in seven minutes. You can do it throughout the day. Whether you're an employee, an entrepreneur, or a creative—or even looking for more connection or clarity in your relationships—you can use Take 7 in any situation.

So, are you ready to go on this journey with me to create more abundance, meaning, and connection in your life? I'm going to be with you every step of the way. I think you're ready to Take 7.

Get ready to go further than you ever thought you'd go.

*Part One*

# Understanding
# Take 7

*Chapter One*

# What's Your Story?

IMAGINE YOU'RE SOMEWHERE NEW. MAYBE AT A networking event in a hotel ballroom, or in a friend's backyard at a child's birthday party, or at a nice restaurant for a business dinner. As you're mingling with strangers and conversations start to brew in that slightly awkward style that happens when people meet, you encounter an enthusiastic listener. She asks, "So, what's your story?" She presses further, "I mean, really, who are you? Tell me your story."

How do you respond? Do you share your relationship status? Tell her about your career aspirations? Talk about the health issues you're dealing with? Sometimes a stranger's question can be just small talk. But sometimes it provokes something bigger.

Deep down, right now you might feel a restlessness stirring. A

3

deep dissatisfaction with the way your career is going. Or frustration with unresolved relationship conflicts. A sense of unease that there's not enough—not enough time, money, or energy. You've tried to shake irritating thoughts or behaviors but just can't seem to let them go. If you were completely honest with this stranger, if you wanted to crash the light banter and make things good and truly weird, you might spill details of confusion or pain or boredom.

Once upon a time you knew what you wanted your life to look like. You had a vision of the career you wanted, the house you'd live in, the partner you'd share a life with, the family you'd build together. Your ideas may have emerged from talents, skills—things you knew you were good at—or from what others expected. You might have considered what your family or teachers said you were destined for. Maybe your vision came from the faith community you were raised in or from observing someone you admired. Maybe you've accomplished a lot of your goals already.

So why don't you feel fulfilled? Why doesn't it feel like you're living the life you were made for?

Your dreams hover just out of reach, the tips of your fingers tingling to touch their elusive edges. Maybe you've bought the latest goal-setting planner and tried daily affirmations. Still, days, weeks, and years go by, and you don't feel any closer to the life you wanted than when you started.

I've been there, friend—unsatisfied with the things I accomplished, reaching for something more that I couldn't define. Those experiences had me stuck, wondering, *Who am I really? How can I become who I've always wanted to be? What have I done that really matters? What difference do I make?*

We tell ourselves a story every day in an attempt to answer those questions. Whether we realize it or not, that story has a powerful impact on our future. Let me geek out on the science here really quick. Neurologists have repeatedly shown that our thoughts can physically alter our bodies.[1] This is because every thought we have is carried by neurotransmitters in our brain, and positive thoughts can release more "feel-good" chemicals, which tangibly impacts our entire body.[2] Our experiences, our perceptions, and our expectations express themselves in how we're wired, down to a cellular level. And the research shows that our minds are wired for stories.[3] Story is how we make sense of what's happening around us, how we see the world.

We're creating stories about our lives all the time. I see this in my coaching business every day. We work out narratives to explain our experiences while also carrying the stories others have told us about who we are and aren't, and what we should do and can't do.

In this book I'm going to challenge you to examine the stories that you've created and get rid of the ones that whisper about your limitations, provoke your fears, and tempt you to apathy.

Let's turn off the white noise drowning out possibility and change and freedom. I think that's what it means when the Bible says, "Keep your heart with all vigilance, for from it flow the springs of life" (Proverbs 4:23). *The springs of life!* I love that phrase! There is so much abundance and joy for you. It's time to stop accepting the crumbs in life.

You can step outside the narrative you've been living and write a new chapter. I know this from personal experience. It wasn't long ago that I found myself living out a narrative that was

I'm going to challenge you to examine the stories that you've created and get rid of the ones that whisper about your limitations, provoke your fears, and tempt you to apathy.

better than I hoped for and yet still not what I deeply desired. So I decided to start a new chapter.

## A Crafted Life

Picture a gigantic palm tree. That's how I remember it, anyway. It was one of my earliest memories. That towering tree had a narrow trunk rising high into the air, with pointy fronds reaching up into the bright blue Southern California sky. It towered over the roof of our house and cast feather-shaped shadows across the lawn.

We were planting yellow and pink flowers. That's the other thing I remember—planting flowers with my dad in the front yard, and the scent of potting soil and wet earth. I was maybe three years old. My dad was strong and healthy, and my parents were still together.

After that my mental movie jumps forward to a surprise birthday party that my dad threw for my mom. I was five. There were colorful balloons, a birthday cake, and lots of friends and family crowded around. I remember feeling so happy. I loved being with people.

That's the last memory I have of my mom, my dad, my brother, and me together—before everything blew apart. Before drug use, rehab, jail, divorce, and financial distress scattered us. The rest of my childhood was crowded out by those realities and their costs. Everything after that felt like it was trying to unsuccessfully balance on a surfboard in a hurricane. And that shift shaped me in many ways.

I'm a fixer by nature, driven to try to right the wrongs around me. Driven to help heal the hurts of people close to me. I became a troubleshooter at a young age. People called me a "wise" child—observant and thoughtful. Those attributes were partly how I'm naturally wired and partly learned survival skills.

As I began to head out into my own life, I knew a couple of things for sure. First, I deeply loved my family of origin. As an adult I could see with greater compassion the many forces that impacted the decisions and challenges that led to a broken home. Second, I knew that I wanted to learn from those lessons and take a different path.

Ironically, I chose a career that was basically a metaphor for my younger life.

I became an ER nurse.

Yep. That's right. Frantically trying to fix things all the time, in intense circumstances, was literally my job. I chose it. And I was good at it. In the ER you never know who you might see next. Your next patient could be a drug addict faking pain and looking for a fix, or it could be a woman who thinks she has severe stomach pains but who is actually nine months pregnant and ready to push. I was good at handling unpredictable circumstances. After all, I'd spent my childhood learning the ropes.

Here's the thing about being an ER nurse: It's noble. It's altruistic. Good nurses are high-capacity people, with a potent blend of compassion and pragmatism. It's important, exhausting, rewarding, and heartbreaking work. I got kudos from friends and family for my career. People marveled that I'd come through a chaotic childhood and made it to functional, contributing adulthood. That in and of itself could be viewed as a miracle.

But something was off. Something in the story of my life

wasn't right. And fixer that I am, I didn't know how to fix it. On the outside it looked like things were going well. And by many definitions, they were. But I wasn't thriving.

Life in the ER has a rhythm and schedule that is grueling under the best of circumstances. The demands of the career are even tougher if something feels off. I was surviving, and I was honored to be part of such important work, but I felt like I was barely hanging on to all my life's responsibilities by my fingernails.

Other nurses around me were living in the fullest realization of who *they* were—completely present during their ER hours *and* loving their off-the-clock time. I found myself wondering, *Why can't I find that balance? Is this how my life is supposed to look? Is this what I studied and sweated and skipped sleep for? Is this who I am destined to be?*

I began to realize that the story I had been writing for myself was going to have to change.

## Taking Back the Narrative

I'm a big reader, so I was fascinated when I learned that many authors scrap portions or even whole first drafts of their books as they're writing and revising. As I learned from writing this one, manuscripts are revised repeatedly before they're published. Can you imagine investing years of writing, money, and resources into a manuscript, then tossing all those pages into a roaring fire?

That's how it can feel when you realize you're not loving how your life's story is turning out. It can be scary. It can feel like a waste. The realization can even produce feelings of guilt or shame.

I needed a different narrative. I needed to discover what wasn't working, what I wanted to change, and why I believed some of the things I believed. I needed to write my own story.

That's how it felt for me. I'd spent so much money and so many years and so much effort putting myself through school. The people around me had watched me do it. They'd praised me for it. I was terrified of letting go of what I'd invested in. I'd made sacrifices in my marriage and given up family time to pursue my chosen profession. Reasonable voices around me said to stick with what I was already doing. They reminded me of the old saying that a bird in my hand—meaning the career and life I was living—was better than the "two in the bush" of any life I might be dreaming about.

Still, I knew it wasn't working. Something in my gut told me this life wasn't my destiny. It wasn't what I *really* wanted.

Fixer that I am, I tried fixing my attitude. I tried fixing my schedule, fixing my hours, fixing my mindset. Still I felt stuck. I needed a different narrative. I needed to discover what wasn't working, what I wanted to change, and why I believed some of the things I believed. I needed to write my own story.

I'd been a good nursing student. Now I started investing that same energy into studying *me*. Studying how to be the best version of me. I read everything on this subject that I could get my hands on, listened to podcasts, and hired coaches. And through all this I began investing in my relationship with myself.

Over time I developed the Take 7 practice. These specific questions provoked me to think in new ways, and the trajectory of my life changed.

My *childhood* set me up for a different story than the one I'm now living. The early days of my *adulthood* were preparation for a far less ambitious story than the one I'm now living. Happily, I'm living way bigger than either of those narratives. I'm living a life of abundance, meaning, and connection. How? I've learned to listen to what I *really* want using Take 7. I do this with intention. I do it regularly. Sometimes I do it multiple times a day.

I'm excited to share this practice with you. These curated questions will help you write the life story that you *really* want. You just have to be willing to answer them honestly. But before we dive deeply into the questions, there's someone you need to meet.

**Your Turn**

# Write the Life Story of Your Dreams

If you're not yet in the process of purposefully writing your story, you're missing out. You're still living a story, but you're passively letting circumstances or other people write it for you. Each of us has done this, by the way, but being passive will not get you the life of your dreams. Only you can determine what your dream life will look like and only you can write that story!

Promise yourself you will pursue the life of your dreams. Then fill in the blanks below.

- The reason it's important to me to know what I really want is

  _____

- When I know what I want, I feel

  _____

- I promise to figure out what I really want by this date:

  _____

## Chapter Two

# Little You

### *Inner Child Work and Why It Matters*

THE PERSON YOU NEED TO MEET BEFORE YOU DIVE into the questions is critical to the Take 7 process. She's been driving a lot of your decisions, avoidances, denials, and coping mechanisms up to this point. She profoundly influences who you are and why you are the way you are.

Who is this person?

It's you. Little You. Your inner child.

What do I mean? There's an inner child inside each of us who holds memories, beliefs, happiness, and hurts. That inner child, Little You, drives more of your motivations than you might think possible. Stay with me for a minute, and let me explain why this is so important.

## The Concept of an Inner Child

The origins of inner child work can be traced back to psychologist Carl Jung. He proposed that we each carry with us a childhood self—meaning, emotions, memories, and experiences.[1] Think about a fully grown tree. If you look at the inside of a tree trunk, you'll see layers upon layers of concentric circles—rings—that mark that tree's many years of growth. Similarly, we have inside us the remnants of the selves we've been in years past. Inner child work focuses on healing and nurturing neglect or woundedness from childhood. Since Jung's time, psychologists and therapists have adopted and built on his writings and ideas, especially when helping adults heal from childhood trauma. I believe everyone can benefit from inner child work.[i]

I was fascinated by what I read about consciousness and the role that subconscious thinking plays in day-to-day life. See, the subconscious mind is formed by age seven. From birth to age seven, we're forming beliefs. The subconscious is essentially formed and closed to new ideas by age twelve. After twelve, core beliefs residing in the subconscious are difficult to change without intention and effort.[2] This is important to understand because 95 percent of our thinking is subconscious.[3] Decision making is profoundly impacted by these thoughts, which were formed when we were basically powerless.

Inner child work gives us an opportunity to tend, champion,

---

i. Inner child work is a deeply personal and individualized process. I'll share deeply from my own inner child work as well as my experience working with thousands of women. That said, I am not a therapist. Mine is a layperson's approach, not a therapeutic approach. So if you've experienced trauma as a child—defined as having experienced highly stressful, frightening, or distressing events—you may find that doing inner child work with the help of a qualified therapist is best for you. I want your experience to be positive and, above all, safe.

and heal the child within so that we can be as healthy and whole as possible. Think about it: as children we were powerless to do much about our circumstances. The adults with the power to help or change our circumstances may have actively or passively neglected to help. When we were experiencing difficulties, they may not have noticed.

The good news is that as adults we do have the power. With intention we can notice and address any needs or hurts that may have gone unnoticed or unaddressed when we were younger. Doing inner child work will also help restore your childlike faith and belief. Remember when you were little and got the question, "What will you be when you grow up?" The sky was the limit! You might have answered that you wanted to be an Olympic gymnast or a veterinarian who also builds skyscrapers. Anything felt possible. You'd dream big without apologizing.

Somewhere along the way, you might have started to listen to voices outside yourself that cast doubts on your dreams, or perhaps failure caused you to question yourself. Doubt is a poison. Questioning yourself can be so toxic. Inner child work restores belief and imagination. You may have felt lost for a while, but after getting in touch with Little You, you'll be able to tap into that amazing potential you've always had.

## "Wait, Cayla. Isn't This a Little Woo-Woo?"

Getting to know Little You may sound woo-woo or overwhelming. It isn't! Loving your inner child is fascinating and powerful work. I've been doing it, and guiding others to do it, for years. It's surprising, it's fun, and it never gets stale. Why? Because each of the women I've helped in this work is a complex, beautiful, and wondrously made person. Getting to see others empowered with this knowledge is an honor and privilege.

Occasionally a woman I'm working with will resist this approach. She might say, "I just want the strategy. I want to get to the next level. I don't need to get into that woo-woo stuff." The reality is that you can have the best action plan in the world to get what you want. You might get the physical things you want in life, but if you don't work on the spiritual and emotional side, you won't be happy. And that's why it's so important to do the physical, emotional, and spiritual work in combination—you're staying true to who God wants you to be while achieving the goals that he's put on your heart. Can you achieve your goals without addressing your inner child? Of course you can. But by doing this work you'll discover the things that hold you back from reaching your full potential. And you can address them and achieve more than you ever dreamed possible.

It can be a total game changer.

Take Jackie for example—mom of four, wife, business owner, daughter, and friend. Jackie flew in to see me for coaching. She'd been super successful in her sales career, but she'd plateaued and wanted to break through to the next level. In our time together we were doing some business strategizing and Jackie was making real progress on that element, but something was holding her back. So I started to ask questions that would help her feel safe to start opening up.

Initially she resisted. I know there's something there whenever

I start noticing resistance. And you might see that with yourself. If you know there's something you don't want to answer, or an area in which you don't want to do the work, there's probably a connected emotion that you don't want to express or a related memory that's struggling to surface. So you just block it off.

As Jackie was answering my questions, we discovered that she had anger and bitterness inside her heart. I assured her we could break through if she did some honest inner child work. She resisted.

I asked, "What scares you so much? What do you think is going to happen when you do this work?"

"I'm afraid to open something that doesn't need to be opened."

I asked, "Can you imagine living a fuller life than you are currently living right now?"

She didn't hesitate. "Yes!"

I suggested that we use the empty chair exercise. It was incredible. Jackie sat in one of three chairs. She imagined Little Jackie sitting in another of the chairs and her dad in the third chair. She accessed all the feelings of being Little Jackie and spoke candidly to her dad. She imagined hearing his point of view too.

This creative act let Jackie express all the things she never got to express—all the things she'd kept pent up inside for years. She got it all out—everything she wanted to say. Then she stood and went to the younger version of herself and spoke to her Little Jackie, saying the things she'd wanted to hear as a child.

She realized she had been stuck as an adult because she'd been seeking her father's approval and permission for years. Once she'd nurtured her inner child, adult Jackie realized it was more than okay to achieve more than her dad had. She was freed up to accomplish more than he'd ever dreamed for himself and far more than he'd ever dreamed for her.

By the end of our time together Jackie had created an additional income stream. She was embracing what's possible—abundant living spiritually, emotionally, and physically.

What happened with Jackie can happen for you. Are you ready to get to know Little You?

## Reacquainting Yourself with Little You

What can I say about Little You? Little You is curious. She has lots of energy, loves with her whole heart, and possesses a big imagination. She's not like anyone else—she's super special. The only problem is that her power is limited. Some places, people, things, and even ideas exist just beyond her reach. The restrictions and the messages from the adults around her limit her. People with power don't always notice or respond to her needs.

Then Little You grew up. You made friends, formed relationships, and learned new skills. You got an education, cultivated talents, fell in and out of love. You tried new places and food. You got smarter, wiser, and more resourceful. Still, the lessons you learned and the messages you received during your childhood stayed with you. Unresolved emotional issues from childhood can impact your thoughts, emotions, and behaviors. Your childhood experiences shaped your beliefs about yourself, others, and the world around you.

Those lessons and messages echo into your today, especially in your subconscious. When you are oblivious to Little You, her

Unresolved emotional issues from childhood can impact your thoughts, emotions, and behaviors. Your childhood experiences shaped your beliefs about yourself, others, and the world around you.

cries for survival, acceptance, love, and nurturing echo in the back of your mind. If you try to silence that voice, you'll find she can throw you off your path again and again.

There are all kinds of ways Little You shows up in relationships, in your self-esteem, and in your emotional responses. Here are some ways you may struggle:

- **Self-Sabotage.** That's Little You who is scared of being rejected. If you dealt with rejection, neglect, or abandonment, you may avoid putting yourself out there.
- **Knowing What You Really Want.** That's Little You who doesn't want to rock the boat or get in trouble and who is looking for approval and wants to please the "grown-ups."
- **Constant Conflict.** That's Little You seeking attention in any way she can. To her, being called dramatic is better than being ignored. (I can say that's a category I fall into all the time, 100 percent.)

Here's the thing. There's not just one version of Little You. There are lots of them. My friend, the psychotherapist Dr. Jenn Chrisman, gave me a word picture that I think is super helpful when it comes to inner child work. Imagine all the past versions of you, from every age and stage of your life up until now. Imagine all those versions of Little You on a bus. The best version of you, your wisest self, is driving. Let's call her your champion self. She knows what she wants and knows how to get there. That's why she's in the driver's seat. She's driving you to the life of your dreams. Powerful image, right?

In a stressful situation, if you're triggered or offended easily, check the driver's seat. When you make emotional, upset decisions, that's not your champion self driving. So ask yourself, *Which version of me is trying to drive right now? Why is she trying to take control?* There's a reason Little You is showing up. It's self-protection.

I imagine myself in a Mercedes G-wagon—it was my dream car for years. (It's actually what I drive now.) I visualize all the past versions of me heading toward my dream life in that blue G-wagon with my best, most fully realized Cayla driving. Young-mom Cayla is strapped in the back seat next to four-year-old Cayla in her booster seat, and charge nurse Cayla is in the third row, backseat driving as usual. The younger versions of yourself shouldn't be in the driver's seat. Your champion self should be driving because you make better decisions, possess greater self-compassion and self-acceptance, and find healing when you acknowledge those past versions of yourself and keep them in their proper place.

As you imagine your champion self taking control of the wheel, get creative. Maybe your vehicle is a Porsche, a minivan, or even a yacht! Use whatever vehicle you like. You may find that your vehicle holds deep meaning for you. A mentor of mine once said, "Cayla, you're driving through life like a bulldozer, and you're meant to be a Ferrari." The more I thought about me as a bulldozer, the more I realized how true that was. The bulldozer version came out when I was living out of fear. When I thought there wasn't enough for me, I pushed my way through. The question was, would I stay in the driver's seat of the bulldozer? Or switch to a Ferrari? I eventually chose to be a G-wagon. You choose whatever you want!

It's fun to visualize this way and it can be so helpful. Visualizing expands your thinking and allows your imagination space to play, a chance to grow.

## Hello, Little Me

Now that you understand how important Little You is to Take 7, how do you get in touch with her? I'm glad you asked.

Let's start right now.

Take a few minutes and get to a quiet spot. Someplace where you can think without interruption. Get comfortable. Relax your shoulders and release any tension you sense in your body. Take a deep breath, breathing in as deeply as you can. Hold that breath for a few seconds, and then release your breath. Stretch your arms and neck. Do that again. And once more.

Ready?

Think back to the home where you grew up. Imagine walking up the path to the front door. Notice what color the door is, what the entrance looks like. Reach for the doorknob. Open that door and recall the scent of your home. Feel the air inside. Is it warm or cool? Is it bright inside or is it dark? Spend a moment taking in the entrance and the rooms just beyond.

Now turn your mind's eye to the hall that leads to your childhood room. Begin walking down there. Notice the pictures on the wall, the color of the paint, the feel of the floor beneath your feet. Soon you arrive at your bedroom door.

Slowly open that door. And picture the room.

On the bed is . . . you. Little You. Visualize your childhood self, sitting there on the bed. What do you look like? What are you wearing? Notice your hair, your skin, your posture. What are you doing?

Watch Little You turn to you. Gently ask her, "What are you feeling? What do you want me to know?"

And now . . . listen.

Does Little You feel loved? Why or why not? Does she feel safe? What does she want? What makes her happy? Does she feel like she belongs, or does she feel at the edge of the crowd? What is she proud of? What is she ashamed of? Where does she feel afraid? Where is she brave? What does she want you to know?

She doesn't need to give you the answers to all these questions. Whatever she decides to tell you in this moment is what she wants you to know. You have the opportunity right now to love on Little You. Regardless of how others treated Little You once upon a time, you can love her well. And that makes more of a difference than you'll be able to grasp. And this is more important even than her talking to you. It matters that you're there to love on her.

What does she need you to say? Maybe she needs to hear, *I see you. I hear you. I love you. Everything will be okay.*

You'll know what she needs when you listen to and acknowledge her. You'll know what makes her tick and what makes her scared and what makes her feel loved. Sit with her. Talk to her. Tell her that you understand. Tell her that you want to do all you can today to help her feel safe and loved. That's what parenting Little You looks like.

*Parenting* is a word that gets loaded up with all kinds of negativity. Ultimately the way I see it is that parenting is about being the adult in the relationship. That doesn't just mean paying for things, running carpool, and cleaning up puke. It's also the unique privilege of knowing someone so intimately that you laugh at the same jokes, sing (badly) together at the top of your lungs without apology, and know when to offer a hug without a word.

You may believe your parents parented you well. Or you might feel like you weren't loved and nurtured in the way you should have been, or the way you'd have liked. It's possible there's an "and" between those two: they parented as best they could *and* you wish they'd done better.

The point isn't to place blame or point the finger at someone else. It is the opposite—it's about recognizing your own agency. It's realizing that right here and right now, you can acknowledge your own feelings. You can actively participate in your own well-being, to receive the grace of God and be stronger and more courageous as a result. What a fabulous opportunity!

Little You needs to know that you haven't abandoned her. You remember her and care for her and you're looking out for her. This is your time to reunite with yourself, to have a homecoming with your closest friend. It's time to lovingly get honest—with your whole self.

## Talking to Yourself

Talking to yourself might sound silly or weird, and I get that. It might feel awkward at first, but remember that reading was awkward when you first tried it. You can talk to yourself however it feels most comfortable for you. Talk to yourself in the mirror. Or write a letter to Little You. Speak to her out loud in the car like you're talking on the phone. Maybe typing notes in an app on your phone will work best for you. There's no right or wrong way to do this.

Being reunited with Little You is cause for celebration. She dreamed big and you get the joy of realizing those dreams with and for her! As kids we could only dream about the things we can now do as adults.

Judy is a great example of this. She was obsessed with horses as a child. She read books about horses, drew thousands of pictures of them, and dreamed of the day she'd go riding. When she bought a horse as an adult, it was the fulfillment of so many dreams. Her inner child feels fulfilled as Adult Judy spends time with her horse, which makes her joy that much fuller.

And there's Annie. Annie brought home a bike with a basket in front and rode it around the block. Her daughter asked, "Mom, is that for me?" Annie smiled and said, "It's for Little Me! But we can share!" Laugh and joke with Little You. She laughs at your jokes when nobody else does!

My Little Me knows what's important to me. She knows things no one else knows—the moments of pride and the wins and the secret fears. She remembers being terrified to perform in a play at camp—and how afterward, she felt like a superstar! Only Little Me has access to my memories—nobody else in my life can provide that perspective.

We'll return to our inner child over and over in this book. As we move through Take 7, we'll be checking in with her, noticing when she pops up with requests or demands, and when she retreats. We'll notice her strong feelings and reactions. Little You will realize that as you go through the questions, you are looking out for her, are thankful for her, are proud of her, and love her.

And in return you will find that you can move forward in a way that incorporates your whole self.

Incorporating your whole self is living authentically—and it's the secret to true breakthroughs. You'll discover greater awareness for why you make decisions the way you do, why you long for certain things, why you get stuck, and what will set you free to go after what you *really* want.

All from making Little You your best friend again.

## Certified Influencer

If you're resisting inner child work because you're afraid it's not Christian, think again. Faith doesn't mean you close your mind or repress your creativity. That's not faith. That's religion. Jesus had a lot of conflict with the religious leaders of his day for good reason: they wanted to maintain the status quo to maintain their own power. I'm not about maintaining the status quo. I'm not religious. I'm a believer.

It breaks my heart to see women settling for less than abundant life. They're missing out on what God has for them. And it also hurts because when you play really big with your life, it gives God a chance to show up and show off. When you only take the safe choice with predictable outcomes, there's no room for letting God show off in your life. When you invite God to show up big, so many lives are improved and changed for the better.

Let me tell you a story. I was about four or five years old and riding in our Mazda minivan with my parents. We lived in a not-nice area of town. One day we drove by Canyon Hills, a big, beautiful church. In a sort of offhanded way, my dad said, "We should start going to church." I could tell my mom was hopeful about that idea.

One night, not long after that, my dad didn't come home. My mom got into that same Mazda minivan with me and my brother in the back seat. Together we drove to all the construction sites in town, trying to find him. It turned out that even though he said he was working, he wasn't. He was doing drugs. Later, when we'd given up looking, he finally came home. My mom told him, "You have to go to rehab."

It was a scary time for our family because we didn't know if he was going to get better or not. We all went to Canyon Hills together when he got out of rehab. It became our church. My parents ultimately got divorced because my dad couldn't kick the habit, but through it all that church was our safe place—our refuge. We were there Sundays and Wednesdays, and that community helped so much during a really hard time.

So at a very young age I saw the power of being with people who love God. I saw how caring they were. They were so kind to me and my little brother and my mom. I wanted to be like that. The church and the way those people embraced and empowered us made a big impact on me.

It wasn't the church that saved me, though. God saved me. He had his hand of favor on me. Even with all we were going through, I never got into trouble. The stereotypical story is that kids who come from broken homes and go through tough circumstances act out, get hooked on drugs, are promiscuous, all that kind of stuff. God protected me from that. I never wanted to do any of those things.

Since the subconscious mind is formed before you're seven years old and closes around age twelve, I am grateful I was grounded in the faith early on. Ever since I was a kid, I've believed God loves us no matter what and he protects and guide us.

I love Jesus. I follow his way. He's my guiding light in everything I do. I have a hunger for God's Word. I memorize and pray the Scriptures. And I know that God's Holy Spirit lives inside me, helping me seek to know God's will for me. One of my favorite verses is this: "Be transformed by the renewal of your mind" (Romans 12:2). Growing and challenging my thinking is a big part of being a believer. This is true for you too. Going after what you *really* want can be transformational work.

God has big plans for each of us. We're called to a life of abundance, not one of scarcity. So why do we settle for so much less?

That's why you're here, reading this. To step into abundance. To fulfill your purpose. Because make no mistake: you were made on purpose for a purpose.

You may be thinking, *Sure. I'm special. I know that. But I can't do* _____ .

Listen, nothing is impossible with God. He can do anything. He created and literally runs this universe. He has done everything for you. His mercies are new every morning (Lamentations 3:23). He's working everything for your good, for his glory. He explicitly tells us to ask for what we want (James 4:2).

He's waiting for you to ask. Are you ready for that?

## Empowered and Ready

Will inner child work be life-changing? Yes. Absolutely. Will it be scary? Maybe a little. But mostly you can think of inner child

God has big plans

for each of us. We're

called to a life of

abundance, not

one of scarcity. So

why do we settle

for so much less?

work as a new pair of glasses. You'll be surprised at how much clearer things are when you do the work!

New ideas are always a little scary at first. But there's no reason to fear. Jesus promised his peace and his presence when the world delivers trials and challenges. "When," not "if." That peace is no joke—it's a promise. And it's not from me—it's from him.

If you're still thinking inner child work and Take 7 is a little woo-woo, consider this: when you are living your best life and living in abundance, all that glory goes to God. He gets the glory! Who doesn't want that?

As you open yourself up to learning more about Little You, you'll see and understand how her voice matters. You'll see why her influence speaks into the dreams and goals you long for. You'll see why you sometimes get stuck. Your growing compassion for Little You will bring deeper compassion for others too.

Some people resist inner child work because they think they don't need help. They might resist therapy. They might think meditation is wrong. Or that visualization is wrong. God gave us an imagination. It's up to us to use what we've been given for good and not for evil.

This will be controversial, but I honestly believe that deliberately not living out an abundant life is wrong. It takes faith to go after an incredible life. Remember, you are what you think. And belief—faith—can move mountains.

It's time to bring your whole self into alignment—mind, body, and spirit. Not just the you of yesterday or today or tomorrow. Your *whole* you.

Now that you know how important this inner child work will be, let's talk about your greatest asset as you realize abundance, meaning, and connection.

**Your Turn**

## Show Her Love

1. Find a picture of your younger self. Choose a baby picture, a picture from your grade school years, a snapshot from your teens, or even an image from your early adulthood—whatever picture or age speaks to your heart.

2. Put it somewhere you'll see it daily. You can make that picture of Little You your screensaver on your phone or frame it and display it in your home. You can even slide it into this book!

3. Look at it often to remind yourself to honor Little You.

# Chapter Three

# You Are Your Biggest Asset

WHEN I WAS BUILDING OUT MY BUSINESS, I ACCU-
mulated some significant savings. I wanted to hire a coach, but
real estate seemed like a safer bet. So I went to my mentor and
asked his advice. I said, "I have this money I want to invest. What
should I do with it?" To my surprise, he didn't skip a beat. He
said, "Invest it in yourself." He affirmed what I knew in my gut
I wanted to do. I hired a coach, and it was the best money I've
ever spent. That investment will be paying me dividends for the
rest of my life.

You are your biggest asset. Whatever assets or liabilities you
have in your portfolio, nothing you have is more valuable than

*you*. I'm not advising that everyone should do exactly what I did. I'm saying that you need to start thinking of yourself as your greatest asset and do the work to grow and love yourself more and more today!

## Grow Your Asset

I am passionate about real estate. I grew up in rentals, so purchasing rental properties and then pouring time, money, and care into them to make them beautiful, comfortable spaces for renters feels extra good. It's one of my favorite ways of generating wealth. When I add amenities—like a pool and lovely landscaping—it brings me joy *and* increases my asset's value.

When you invest in yourself, you'll grow. That might look like hiring a coach to help you elevate or reading this book or taking a class. The returns on the knowledge you gain will pay off forever and ever. You control the level of investment, which means you control your potential.

## Protect Your Asset

When it comes to my real estate assets, any potential renters go through a background check and provide references. To protect our greatest asset, we need to create healthy boundaries.

You'll have to decide what and who you let in. You're going to new heights in your life. You'll have to say no. A lot. That will tick some people off. Maybe even a lot of people. Boundaries bug those who don't have enough self-love to have boundaries for themselves. Just know this: when people get mad, it's confirmation that you're going places.

According to Dr. Jolene Brighten, neglecting your needs messes with your hormone balances and contributes to a host of illnesses and symptoms.[1] Is it any wonder so many of us are sick? I invited Dr. Brighten on my podcast. Since she's a medical doctor, it really struck home with me when she gave this bit of advice: "Unapologetically prioritize your needs and the things that make you feel good and bring joy." I can't argue with that!

It matters who you surround yourself with. Who's speaking into your life? Who in your community helps build up your faith? Who do you spend time interacting with socially? Are the people you're hanging out with feeding your spirit or are they stealing your joy?

Recently I had to decide—for myself—what's acceptable for me. I got honest about what wasn't working for me. I set some boundaries. Choosing to limit my association with certain people who used to have full access to my heart was tough at first, but it has been so helpful. I still love those people. My boundaries just help me love them *wisely*.

People got mad at Jesus when he was on earth, on mission. His essence, his clarity, challenged them. To be with him, they had to either level up or step off. Many chose to step off. Those who stuck by him were inspired and forever changed. Keep leaning in, keep going forward and moving in the direction of your vision.

## **Think Big**

People will say they want you to be successful—until it affects them. Somebody in your life won't like seeing you living your truest design by God. Your new boundaries will affect their life-style. They'll prefer you to stay the way you've always been. That's more comfortable for them. If they pull you down, that's not love. That's the opposite of love. (See 1 Corinthians 13 for the true definition of love!)

Take Jeannie for example. She had a great sense of style, but her job didn't pay well. She wanted to create extra income, so she started creating videos where she put together outfits on a budget that she posted online. Soon her dream was becoming a reality. Multiple makeup and fashion brands offered her deals. It was exciting! She was on the cusp of transforming her life and her family's lives by creating passive income.

Then her hometown friends and family discovered her feed. They posted, "Who do you think you are?" Strangers on the internet were showing her more love and appreciation than her so-called friends. Her self-esteem couldn't take it. She deleted her social media account. Jeannie had so much potential, yet she refused to push through the resistance to get what she *really* wanted. It was like she'd custom ordered a gourmet meal for delivery, perfectly cooked and paid for, but when the doorbell rang, she refused to answer.

Some overcome resistance; most don't. They use their voices until they're challenged and then they go silent. They go back to what they've always done. And I can relate. I almost did that too.

When I started to build my brand on social media, people

close to me said, "You've changed." And in a way it was true. Even though I was still me, I was becoming a better version of me! I had more wisdom, more strength, and a desire to teach people—I hadn't always had that. The resistance said, "Shrink, go back to who you used to be." And I almost gave up.

That season taught me a lesson I'll never forget. If you're going to do anything meaningful in this world, you're not going to be universally liked. People will hate you. People will love you. You get to decide if you're going to succumb or shine.

I realized those who couldn't handle my shine had to go. It's not important that everyone like me. What's important is that I step into my God-given destiny. I won't give up on God's design for me or giving him the glory. There is some grief around that loss, but I know it's better to shine than to succumb. I dream big, and that means sometimes I get some hate for it.

Let's be clear: loving yourself isn't enabling. It isn't license to do the wrong things over and over and over again. Love recognizes we're called to a higher standard. Loving yourself well means constantly stretching, constantly challenging yourself to growth and renewal. Ultimately that true, authentic, God-given self-love allows us to be more Christlike.

## The Freedom Wheel

Part of loving yourself is getting super honest about the current quality of your life. A great way to do this is to perform a life audit, going through seven important areas of your life, which I think of as the seven spokes of what I'll call the Freedom Wheel.

Loving yourself well

means constantly

stretching, constantly

challenging yourself to

growth and renewal.

Ultimately that true,

authentic, God-given

self-love allows us to

be more Christlike.

If all these areas are at optimal health, you're living a full, abundant life.

1. Health: _____
2. Wealth: _____
3. Career: _____
4. Spiritual Life: _____
5. Romantic Life: _____
6. Family Life: _____
7. Social Life: _____

I challenge you to take time to do a life audit right now, rating your satisfaction in every area on a scale of 1–10 with 1 being unhappy and 10 being thriving. Rank these categories leading with your strongest. The last will be the area you feel is your weakest. Remember you're in a safe space and this is just for you—nobody will judge you for this.

Each of these areas influences the others. Sometimes a high level of focus on one area can lead to imbalance. Take me for example. For a period in my life, I was such a high achiever that I was not protecting my health. Especially during the ten years when I sold health and wellness supplements, my body was my business. I was secretly terrified I would lose my business if I gained weight. I was telling myself this story that I had to be skinny and high energy, or I'd be poor. I carried around a lot of stress about having to look and act a certain way. The consequence was that I basically burned out my adrenals and was diagnosed with adrenal fatigue in 2019. That was a reality check and gave me a chance to reevaluate my priorities.

Now I'm super intentional about taking care of my health. Living healthily and aging well is a priority, so I invest time, money, and resources in my health, just as I would invest in my real estate properties. I have a concierge doctor who helps me reach my health goals.

When it comes to my most recent life audit, as I look at the Freedom Wheel, I'm working on these goals:

1. **Health:** Sleeping eight hours a night.
2. **Wealth:** Growing my real estate fund.
3. **Career:** Executing a successful book launch.
4. **Spiritual Life:** Connecting with God and others at Monday and Friday Bible studies.
5. **Romantic Life:** Going on more date nights with my husband.
6. **Family Life:** Practicing better boundaries.
7. **Social Life:** Spending intentional time with true friends.

After you've rated yourself on the Freedom Wheel, determine your intentions in each area. Imagine your limitless potential. State what that reality will look like in present tense, for instance:

1. **Health.** I sleep eight hours a night and wake feeling refreshed and restored.
2. **Wealth.** I'm helping one hundred investors in my real estate fund.
3. **Career.** My book is a bestseller.
4. **Spiritual Life.** The Bible study I participate in weekly deepens my faith.

5. **Romantic Life.** Weekly date nights with my husband help me connect with him and feel seen.
6. **Family Life.** I enjoy spending scheduled time with my family.
7. **Social Life.** True friends know and support me as I support them.

What are your current goals and intentions in more fully developing each area?

1. **Health.** _____
2. **Wealth.** _____
3. **Career.** _____
4. **Spiritual Life.** _____
5. **Romantic Life.** _____
6. **Family Life.** _____
7. **Social Life.** _____

## Energy Leaks

As babies, we naturally expressed our needs and desires. We cried when we were sad or hurting. If we were hungry, we ate. But as we grew up, we lost touch with our needs and feelings. Our natural impulses were trained out of us. (I hope I'm teaching my children better—we'll see.)

Neglecting your needs will create an energy leak. If you don't process emotions, you stuff them or compartmentalize them.

That survival technique can work in the short term, but it's not effective or helpful for long periods of time. Say, for example, you've got a sick kid at home and you're in crisis mode, but in the back of your mind you have an unexpressed concern about your marriage. That issue is placed on the back burner while you handle the immediate priorities of a sick child. You plan to handle that marriage problem when there's time or energy. You think, *When everything settles down, I'll deal with my concerns about my marriage. Are we gonna make it? Will our marriage survive? I'll think about that later.* You're not *consciously* thinking about those questions. You're dealing with the immediate issue. It's your subconscious that's worried, and that's causing an energy leak.

As I was working on this chapter, I had to check myself on this, reminding myself to protect my biggest asset. I was leaking energy and losing steam and I didn't know why. Revenue was down in one of my businesses. It had been declining for months. I felt the impact and my team did too. And here's the thing: *I had this story in my mind that I was disappointing them.* I wanted to take care of the members of that team. So I spent time and energy and money scrambling around trying to reinvigorate that piece of the business.

I was hitting a wall. My energy is usually high and I'm good at creative thinking, but I was depleted. The solution wasn't coming to me. Plus I was crying. When I'm not dealing with something in my life, I cry easily about little things. We all have those tells, right? When I started to cry over something small, I got curious. What was going on?

Then it hit me: I needed to go through Take 7 for this situation. So I did, and it took only thirty minutes to create clarity. I knew what my next step was. It would be hard, but I knew what I had to do.

Here's what it looked like when I coached myself through Take 7 for this issue.

1. **What's not working for me in my life?** I'm telling myself a story in which I am responsible for everyone's happiness. Now I am depleted and feel like a failure.

2. **When did I first start accepting that?** After my dad went to jail, I worried that if things got too hard for my mom, she'd abandon me too. I decided it was my job to make things easier for her so she wouldn't leave me.

3. **What Little Me is showing up right now?** What does she need to hear? A tired version of my ten-year-old self is showing up. She needs to hear that her peace, her joy, and her comfort matter. I love her. I will care for her and not let her be exhausted and feel neglected.

4. **What's a better way of looking at this?** I can remind myself that I've learned a lot doing what I can in this space, and it served us all for a time. I had so much fun and I made a lot of money.

5. **Where is there space for gratitude in this?** I can express gratitude for the people who've worked on this team and the financial provision and life experience this has provided for us.

6. **What do I really want?** I really want to focus on my real estate fund. I want space to reimagine the possibilities for my platform and not spin my wheels on this thing that's no longer useful to me.

7. **What is the best next step for me?** Time for some tough conversations. I will no longer actively promote this part of the business. I can empower the team members with a choice about how to proceed and clearly communicate a boundary: I won't be pouring resources into this area anymore.

By actively coaching myself through Take 7, I was protecting my biggest asset: me! I took some time with my team and told them I was experiencing an energy leak. It was time to stop the leak and replenish myself.

It wasn't easy. My answers to the Take 7 pointed me in the direction of a difficult step. Having those hard conversations wasn't fun. I feel vulnerable even writing about it now. I would have preferred to spare myself that anguish and not go through any of that, but my definition of success—doing what I want, when I want, with whom I want—guides me. Walking through that prepared me for what's next. And now that I've taken that action, I'm loving what's next.

So, what will you do with your biggest asset? What's your investment strategy?

## Access Is Everything

We have access to the greatest power in the universe! God wants to help us, but we can be so stubborn. It's up to us to believe his promises. Maybe you're believing lies about God. See, you experience the God you believe in. What God are you believing in? This is worth exploring. Is the God in your mind a big, scary god bent on punishing you for not following rules? Are you imagining a withholding parent who bribes you and punishes you? That will lock you up for sure. That kind of belief leads to a lot of fear and doubt.

In my experience, a woman's beliefs about God often correlate with her experience with her earthly father or father figure. Since beliefs drive behavior on a subconscious level, intellectually you can know God is good yet on a subconscious level still believe he's not.

For instance, my dad wasn't around much when I was young. I tried to get him to come around by achieving and performing. I was always striving. Even as an adult I sometimes catch myself trying to attract God's favor with my accomplishments. When that happens, I'm projecting my beliefs about my earthly father onto my view of God. Now that I'm more aware of these unconscious beliefs driving my behavior, I am rewiring my thinking, replacing negative thoughts with the truth.

Take a few minutes to think about how you'd describe your father. Some words I've heard from clients include "distant," "hard to please," "sarcastic," "critical," "funny," "reckless," "needy," "pushy," "kind," "forgiving," "ignorant," and "well educated." There are no wrong answers here. But not all these words accurately describe the God of the Bible.

God is great, magnificent, the Creator, a miracle maker, the beginning and the end—the Alpha and Omega—a loving Father! God is the author of all, the giver of all, and God is love. God is life. He is the God of abundance. He created this entire universe. God made you in his image.

It is our birthright to walk in abundance. He gives us access

Since beliefs drive

behavior on a

subconscious level,

intellectually you

can know God

is good yet on a

subconscious level

still believe he's not.

to everything that contributes to abundance: well-being, peace, purpose, progress. And abundance is God's plan for you. Not scarcity. He's about abundant life, including salvation, nourishment (spiritual food), healing, and quality of life. Anytime you see lack—stealing, killing, and destruction—that's from the Enemy, not from God.

Begin to see abundance as an inheritance from your Father—not just as a "someday in heaven" idea but rather as a characteristic of your life right now. Maybe you look at what you have and think, "How can God make abundance out of this?" I have some math for you: 2 loaves + 5 fish = 5,000 people fed. He took two loaves and five fish and fed five thousand people (John 6:5–13). Again and again during his earthly ministry, Jesus reminded us not to focus on our resources but rather concentrate on making the next right move.

God also loves it when we take the next step in faith. Again and again in Scripture we hear this encouragement:

> Do not despise these small beginnings, for the LORD rejoices to see . . . the plumb line in Zerubbabel's hand.
>
> —ZECHARIAH 4:10 NLT

> Well done, good and faithful servant. You have been faithful over a little; I will set you over much.
>
> —MATTHEW 25:23

By being faithful in the small things, you participate in abundance.

He will make a way.

He'll make a way for abundance in your relationships too. So many women struggle with creating true, deep connections. I'm not talking about surface acquaintances that never really get deeper—I'm talking about friends you can count on and depend on and do life with. That's part of an abundant life. God wants deep, abiding connections for you. He's wired you to long for that in your relationships. And he's ready to give you the desires of your heart.

Most assets have limited potential. What's great about being your own biggest asset is that you have *limitless* potential. In the next chapter we'll look at how your greatest asset—*you*—can be held back by believing some limiting lies, and we'll also examine what you can do to unlock your limitless potential.

## Dream Life

Your biggest asset has unlimited potential in terms of your health, wealth, career, spiritual life, romantic life, family life, and social life.

- What would it look like to be completely unlimited in each area?

- What would life look like if you had endless resources of time and money?

- What's holding you back in each area? Write it out in the present tense.

  - Health: _____
  - Wealth: _____
  - Career: _____
  - Spiritual Life: _____
  - Romantic Life: _____
  - Family Life: _____
  - Social Life: _____

*Chapter Four*

# From Limiting Beliefs to Unlimited Potential

IMAGINE A TINY, FURRY BUNDLE OF ENERGY THAT could fit inside your purse—that's Bentley, our adorable Cavapoo puppy. I love hanging out with Bentley. As tiny as he is, he thinks he's invincible. He will try to eat anything, chase after any potential "prey" (even our neighbor's cat), and explore anywhere without fear.

We were all little Bentleys once. Until we grew up. Along the way we took on what psychologists call "limiting beliefs"—the thoughts, states of mind, or beliefs that artificially hold us back from what we want or need.[1] Most of the time we are completely unaware that we're held back by these artificial limits because they're woven deep in our subconscious.

Through the rest of this book as you discover what you really want by working through Take 7, you will also encounter some of your limiting beliefs. The good news is, with your champion self in the driver's seat, you can challenge these limits and choose what you believe. Let me share with you some examples of how limiting beliefs come into play.

## Limiting Versus Limitless Beliefs

### BELIEF #1

Limiting belief: It's hard to make money.
Limitless belief: Money comes easily when you're in your zone.

Linda was making six figures a year in the medical field when we started working together, but that career and income weren't what she really wanted. She had a deep desire to be a millionaire. As we worked through Take 7, she realized a limiting belief she'd held for a long time. Her mom came from a wealthy family but had been cut off from that wealth. As a result, Linda grew up hearing her mom complain about not having enough money.

Linda got a job in the corporate world to have a steady income. For years she worked long hours at a job she didn't love. Working through Take 7, she realized she had a limiting belief. That was the turning point for her. She had been telling herself, *It's hard to make money*. That was the artificial limit she'd placed on her potential.

Together we found many examples of women all over the world making lots of money. She read their stories. Many were multimillionaires who'd launched their own businesses—which was exactly what Linda wanted to do. She created a whole new business, using her deep experience in the medical field. She took steps to make her dream a reality, and within eighteen months she became a millionaire.

She got what she really wanted.

## BELIEF #2

Limiting belief: I'm not qualified.

Limitless belief: I'm uniquely qualified!

Erin was a retired attorney who led a coaching business. The business was doing well, but she was limited by her own self-perception. She didn't believe she'd achieved enough success as an attorney to be an authority. That belief was a barrier to her success.

As we worked through Take 7, Erin recalled a critical moment in her career. She'd just come back from maternity leave when a partner in her firm ripped her to shreds, insisting she put in more hours. He told her she'd never get anywhere in her career. She'd felt defeated, like her career was doomed. Now she realized that if she'd had someone like her champion self coaching her back then, it would have meant the world to her. She'd have learned how to survive and thrive. Those difficulties had, in fact, qualified her. Her experiences led to her amazing coaching abilities. Erin recognized her limiting belief of "I'm not qualified" and turned it into the limitless belief of "I'm uniquely qualified."

Erin now hosts amazing retreats, empowering attorneys like her younger self to overcome challenges in the workforce.

## BELIEF #3

Limiting belief: I don't know what to do.
Limitless belief: The answers are inside me.

When Ashley started working with me, she had a great idea for an e-commerce business. She'd just sold her previous company, so she had capital to invest in her idea. The trouble was that she believed she did not know what to do. She'd never started a jewelry line before.

I challenged her limiting belief with the proof that she did know what to do. After all, she had sold a ton of other consumer products online. Ashley got curious, trying to figure out where this idea of not knowing what to do had originated. She remembered stalling on a project in high school because she didn't have guidance. She'd received a failing grade.

To give her conscious mind proof that she did know what to do, Ashley pulled up the marketing plan she'd created for her jewelry line, along with her profit and loss plan. She treated herself like a potential investor and sold herself on the idea.

Her new limitless belief? *I know what to do.* The answer was already inside her.

## BELIEF #4

Limiting belief: I'm a victim.
Limitless belief: I'm an overcomer.

My car got broken into twice when I was in nursing school. According to the police report, I was a "victim" of robbery. The first time, my purse, my passport, and all the gift cards I'd been given at my wedding were stolen. Sentimental things I'd kept in that purse were gone forever. I was devastated! On top of that, my car windows were broken, so I had to pay for them to be fixed. *Why me?*

The second time my car was broken into, the thieves got nothing. I'd figured out that leaving my valuables in the car wasn't smart. I could have focused on my loss and feeling helpless, but instead I chose to learn and better protect myself in the future. If you accept that you are powerless, you may reinforce that with the language you use. Your champion self takes radical responsibility for the results in your life.

## BELIEF #5

Limiting belief: I don't have time.
Limitless belief: I make time for what's important to me.

Single mom and business owner Robin identified a desire to grow in her social life as she worked through Take 7. But between her work and her family, her calendar was full. Once she recognized her desire and the limiting belief holding her back from what she really wanted, she audited her calendar. Robin had been using her lunch break to work out. So she decided to view that hour with a new perspective. She reached out to women she'd identified as potential mentors and invited two of them to walk with her once a week. After they met, they agreed to meet the next week. Over the next year, the trio developed a relationship that now provides a loving support system.

Time is a precious resource. How you spend it is up to you. When you recognize that you have the power to control your time your way, the possibilities are endless!

Your champion

self takes radical

responsibility

for the results

in your life.

## BELIEF #6

Limiting belief: I shouldn't feel this way.
Limitless belief: Emotions are my superpower.

Emotions aren't right or wrong, they just *are*. We can have feelings and not let them "have" us. Think about that for a minute. You are allowed to feel any kind of way. Feeling your emotions won't harm you or anyone else. Actions can do violence, feelings cannot.

## Emotions Can Limit You

As you work through Take 7, you may need to release some anger, hurt, or sadness. You may have avoided, medicated, pushed down, or pent up some feelings for so long that you feel like a geyser with the potential to go off at any moment. If you're in a safe space to do so, go ahead. Allow your feelings to surface and come out of you. Release them!

Releasing pent-up emotions defuses the feeling of pressure. The only way to get free is to move through. I've worked with so many women who have stuffed or avoided feelings because they thought they should. That's why I developed the following exercise.

In other words, emotions are morally neutral. When we suppress or avoid them, that's what makes us sick. Once we discharge our feelings in a safe place, they lose their power. Defuse them and then you can take intentional action that's in line with what you want—your personal values and goals.

# Emotions Exercise

- List all the emotions a person might experience. I'll get you started:
  - Sad
  - Angry
  - Frightened
  - Joyful
  - Surprised
  - Frustrated
  - Lonely
  - Jealous
  - Anxious
  - Curious
- Circle the emotions that are safe to feel.
- Look again at your list. Now circle the *whole page*.

Why the whole page? Because literally anything you could or will feel is fine! *Feelings aren't right or wrong.* It's what we do that matters.

Instead of ignoring them, if you get curious about your emotions, you can learn a lot about what matters most to you. Take Jesus for example. Look at when he expressed anger. He went into the temple and saw vendors cheating people. He was so angry, he tipped the tables over and told the vendors to get out (Matthew 21:12–13). His anger provoked action. Because he cared deeply, he took action to restore respect for the sacred space of the temple. He faced conflict head-on with the courage of his convictions. It made people want to follow him even more.

How you feel does not determine your reality. It's how you *act* that gets you where you want to go—to the life of your dreams.

## Words Can Limit or Empower

As you go through Take 7, speak kindly to and about yourself. The words you use can either drain you or lift you up. Loving, life-giving words make us feel energized. Studies show that even plants thrive when spoken to lovingly. Plants spoken to with shame and anger decline quickly and even die.[2]

So use the most positive-energy language you possibly can. Refuse to use words that imply victimhood. Choose empowered language that shows you are in charge of your life. For example, instead of "I have to work out" try "I get to work out." That tiny shift from passive to active instantly shifts things. And if you find yourself saying *always* or *never*, try rephrasing to communicate that you're intentionally making progress.

## Negative Words Versus Positive Words

| | |
|---|---|
| I'm always in a rush. | It's time to retool my calendar to create more margin. |
| I could never sell something. | I get to introduce people to the right product to help improve their lives. |
| I never know what to post on social media. | I'm creating a strategy to guide me in what I post. |

# The Limits of "Should"

The last limiting belief to be on the lookout for is the mindset around the word "should." Little You spent a lot of time figuring out what everyone's role was. She might still have rigid beliefs about those roles. If something upsets you or feels off, take note of the "should" statements in your head. Does what you're thinking line up with what's important to you now, as an adult? Only you can decide.

Take my friend Ami for example. When she picked her daughter up from school, her daughter was crying, so Ami asked what was wrong. She said, "You're late again!" Ami felt defensive and started to justify her actions. But she was currently working through Take 7, so she noticed that her daughter felt upset. Then she remembered a time her father had been late to pick her up. She'd felt powerless to change things. She believed children had to put up with late parents. Ami realized that belief wasn't in line with her values—it wasn't what she wanted for herself and her family. So she apologized to her daughter and made a

If something upsets you or feels off, take note of the "should" statements in your head. Does what you're thinking line up with what's important to you now, as an adult?

commitment to be on time for her family. It was a turning point for her—and for her relationship with her daughter.

I identified a limiting belief in my marriage not long ago. I'd tried the affirmation that "I am a good wife," but it wasn't working. My body refused to believe it. So I got honest with myself about what I believed on a subconscious level. I'd been believing that "I don't know how to be a good wife."

I got curious about what I thought a good wife looked like. I imagined the basic, stereotypical housewife I'd seen on television growing up, the one who cooked three meals a day, ironed her husband's clothes, and so on. Then I asked myself, "Is that true? Do those actions reflect my values?" Since my faith is important to me, I read Proverbs 31, a passage in the Bible that describes a worthy wife. Nowhere did I find her ironing clothes and cooking meals. Instead, I saw much of what I was currently doing reflected there. She tends to the hearts of her household, prepares for the future without fear, is a good steward of resources . . . those values aligned with mine. Here was proof for Little Me that I am a good wife. Once I took care of her concerns, my champion self could get back in the driver's seat.

As you notice and nurture your inner child, be on the lookout for any limiting beliefs. Challenge them. When you overcome false limitations and choose what beliefs you want to hold on to, your potential is limitless!

Now, in the next chapter let's dig in to find out what you *really* want.

## Prosperity Walk

Abundance, meaning, and connection are your birthright! Take time today to go on a prosperity walk.

1. Write out what you know to be true about you. (For example: *I'm a child of God. I was made in God's image. The events of my life are happening for me, not to me—for my good.*[3])
2. Record yourself speaking these truths.
3. Listen to those affirming words in your own voice as you take a walk, and let the truth sink in.

*Part Two*

# Applying Take 7

# Chapter Five

# Voice It

## Question 1: What's Not Working for Me in My Life?

What we resist persists.

—CARL JUNG

THE FIRST QUESTION TO ASK YOURSELF WITH THE Take 7 practice is, *What's not working for me in my life?* This question asks you to honestly voice what feels off or out of alignment in your life right now.

Your feelings matter. Your opinions matter. Would you discard or override the feelings and opinions of your child? Your partner or husband? A friend? Let's say someone you care about loves chocolate and is gluten free. Would you bring her a vanilla birthday cake? No, you'd be mindful of what she likes and what keeps her healthy and happy. You'd find her some chocolate-covered strawberries. So why not find out what *you* really want? It's time to use the voice God gave you to articulate your own needs. You get to decide.

You may veer away from honest confession like I used to do, avoiding what isn't working in your life. When I first started doing mindset work, I went through a lot of trouble, twisting and turning around to make every negative into a positive. If I didn't get a good parking space, I'd say, "More steps for me today!" But that can become a crutch. By reading this book you've declared your desire to grow and change. It's time to figure out what's not working for you. Identify your complaint. Once you're clear on exactly what your complaint is and you give yourself the permission to voice it, that knowledge will help you create massive change in your life.

## Voicing Your Complaint (Versus Complaining)

So, how is voicing a complaint different from complaining? Good question! Here are the differences.

- **A complaint is a fact.** When you know something is not right, you voice it and work to come to a solution. For example, say you're out to eat at your favorite restaurant and you order a well-done burger. When the waiter brings your plate, you slice into the burger and the inside is bright pink. What are you going to do? You voice a complaint. "Sir, I asked for my burger to be cooked well-done. Please take this back." You state it with confidence, knowing it's something that can be changed. A complaint communicates, "I deserve more." It's an empowered statement.

- **Complaining is negative and passive.** When you know something isn't right but you have no intention or action plan to correct it, that's complaining. Let's say you're back at your favorite restaurant again and you order your burger well-done, and it once again comes out pink. But this time you don't say anything to the waiter. Instead you try to eat but complain about the order being wrong to the friend who is eating with you. You're playing the victim instead of voicing a complaint to the person who could fix it.

When you're seeking what you *really* want, only voice a complaint that you're willing to do something about. That's the rule. Because when you use your voice to say what's not working in your life, you're making an empowered move.

When I was about ten, we lost our family home. A real estate agent came to look at our house, sizing it up, and soon the bank foreclosed on us. We became renters and each year when our lease expired, we'd move. I felt shame around how we lived.

Those realities and the feelings I had around them shaped a lot of my decisions. I chose to become a nurse in part because I'd heard there was a nursing shortage and that I'd always have a job

When you use
your voice to say
what's not working
in your life,
you're making an
empowered move.

if I was a nurse. My husband, Chase, and I married young and bought our dream home when I was just twenty-five. We soon had two kids under the age of three. Measuring my life against the way I'd grown up, I was a success story. But we were also six figures in debt, living paycheck to paycheck, and my marriage was messy. I felt stuck. So I asked myself, *What's not working for me in this situation?*

The complaint was that I needed more money. But honestly, money wasn't the problem. That was Little Me's fear. More money doesn't always fix problems. Money is great, but if you can't manage one hundred dollars well, you won't be able to manage one thousand dollars much better. When it came to money, I realized I'd been making emotional decisions, throwing money at problems instead of dealing with them. That was my inner child, not my champion self, and that approach landed me in debt.

When it comes to finances, Little Me will captain the ship right into an iceberg. But she didn't need to drive. She needed my attention. I showed her how far we'd come and assured her that she wasn't going to be poor ever again.

It was time for my champion self to decide what was important and go for it. And what I *really* wanted was financial freedom. I challenged myself to go deeper. What would that financial freedom look like for me? If I didn't have a huge mortgage and personal debt tying me to a job that I knew in my gut wasn't my destiny, how would that impact me? What would it feel like to have that freedom? What would I do with it? *Why* was that freedom something I wanted? How did I need to grow and change before I was equipped to live the life I was dreaming about? What would it take to get there?

After getting honest with myself—and Little Me—I saw how my specific life experiences led to unconscious beliefs around money. For instance, Little Me believed that there wasn't enough money to go around. She had a scarcity mentality. As an adult, I've discovered an abundance mentality. I believe there is abundant money. But scarcity beliefs were driving many of my choices and behaviors.

So by voicing my complaint—I need more money—I was able to put my champion self in the driver's seat. I crafted a different version of the future. I began to dream with intention and started taking steps to get there.

## Why Is It Hard to Name What's Not Working?

What's standing in the way of you naming what's not working? I think there are probably a couple of things that could be holding you back and I want to address them head-on.

### WE DON'T WANT TO BE SEEN AS WHINERS

Even super brave and powerful women I've coached may initially resist using their voice this way. They say, *I'm not a whiner. I don't want to complain.* Or *I can handle it. I've always been strong.*

Here's what I tell them. Acknowledging pain, discomfort, dissatisfaction, or disease doesn't make you a whiner. It doesn't mean you are griping. Taking ownership of your feelings and preparing for change is one of the boldest things you can do. You claim power when you answer "What's not working?" You claim your agency. You declare you're able to do something to change your life.

It's the first step to building the life of your dreams. It's a bold step. Reluctance to use your voice will keep you from living that dream life. You can only solve a problem you have acknowledged. Any objections that say your voice doesn't matter—they lie! They're keeping you from living in purpose with love and riches.

You are in a safe place. It is necessary and good to acknowledge what isn't working. In claiming this freedom, you will trust yourself more.

## WE'RE WORRIED ABOUT BEING SELFISH

"Selfishness" is defined as lacking consideration for others. Answering "What's not working for me in my life?" is not selfish. Acknowledging what's not working is a generous act.

Here's why: You live in community. You don't operate in a vacuum. Your unrealized dreams and wasted potential profoundly affect those around you. When you experience personal growth, you're not the only one who gets a lift. So does your family. Your community. Your customers. Your extended family. The people you hire. By living your best life, you create a ripple effect enlarging the health, happiness, and wealth of infinite numbers of people!

## WE'RE MORE COMFORTABLE ADDING SOMETHING TO OUR LIVES

We are conditioned to think adding things to our lives will lead to happily ever after. Instead of being intentional about what is already in our lives, we strive for more, more, more. We think we'll be happy when we get the job, the marriage, the house, the kids, the car, the friends. Right?

But *more* isn't always better. More is just more. Why do we keep adding more without intention? Just because Mary's happy with her country club membership, her golf membership, her PTA leadership, and her nonprofit board seat doesn't mean you will be.

Sometimes we take on *more* because we haven't intentionally thought through our desires. I signed up to be class mom for Cooper's kindergarten class once, thinking I wanted to be that kind of mom. But I'm not. I hated it. I found myself wishing his first school year was over just so I could be done with being room mom! Sad, right? I know! I learned my lesson. That's just not my thing.

## WE HAVE DECISION FATIGUE

You may be reading this right now and you cannot name your complaint. You have what I call decision fatigue. You spend your energy on a thousand little choices that don't matter in the grand scheme of getting what you *really* want. Instead of living in abundance, as you were created to be, you're stuck in decision fatigue.

An article in *Psychology Today* suggests that the average person makes "an eye-popping 35,000 choices per day . . . roughly 2,000 per hour."[1] So many choices can be overwhelming, especially when we don't have clarity about the life we really want.

One compassionate thing I've learned to do is offer myself limited choices. I have routines so that I don't spend needless energy on inconsequential decisions. Then, if I'm feeling stuck on a decision, I take three deep breaths and do one of four things: Move my body. Hydrate. Eat something nutritious. Or do something creative. By giving myself limited choices, I'm acknowledging that my needs matter.

## WE ARE FOCUSED ON PLEASING OTHERS

Pleasing others is often our fallback when we don't have clarity on what we truly want. Instead we let other people's choices override our wants and needs.

Take Jasmine for example. She's got the stunning house with the ocean view, a thriving business, two healthy girls, and a loving husband. She's a walking success story. Women covet what she has. But recently Jasmine told me her complaint. Her kids really wanted a dog. She thought, *I want the kids to be happy*, so she researched the "perfect" family dog. She drove two hundred miles to pick up this special dog that won't make her family sneeze their heads off because they're allergic. She dropped a few thousand dollars on this furry little bundle of joy and brought him into her home.

Guess what? A week later the kids were on to something new, ignoring the puppy. Now she's cleaning up piddles all over her house, chasing this puppy around to keep him from running out into the road, and searching for a doggie handler to help with this new responsibility, wondering, *What have I gotten into?*

Having a dog is a big life decision. Jasmine hadn't taken time to design her dream life. She has what others would call a great life, but when she gets clear on what she wants, she might realize that her dream life includes travel. She made a choice that supported what her kids wanted. It wasn't what she really wanted.

It's time to get clear on what is *not* working for you. What are you experiencing or feeling that is *not* what you want? It's not about being critical or ungrateful. It's about acknowledging and getting *specific* about what is not working.

Show Little You that you're paying attention, that you're not brushing off the signals that your body, mind, and spirit are sending you. Voice your complaint. Take a deep breath and put your hand over your heart and say, "I am safe. I'm allowed to use my voice. My voice matters."

## Use Your Imagination

Imagine a child—they've been quiet in their bedroom for a while. This has you concerned. You knock on the door, and the child invites you in. Now imagine that child inside the room is Little You. She is waiting, quietly hoping to be seen, heard, and loved. Step inside. Be ready to listen to what she says with an open mind and heart.

Little You will help you identify what's not working for you. As adults we will lie to everyone around us and say that everything's okay. Our marriage is fine. Our business is fine. Our friendships are fine. Our family is fine. Our spiritual life is fine. And we can consciously believe the lie because we're saying it so much.

But deep down inside, our inner child knows something's off, even though we may not have put a finger on it yet. That inner child knows, *Something's not working for me here.* Give yourself space to go through what's not working for you in your health, wealth, career, spiritual life, romantic life, family life, and social life.

Little You knows when you're being honest. She knows when you're hiding something. You might paste on a smile and act brave for those around you, you might pretend and fool everyone. But deep inside, Little You is not fooled. She knows when something's not right.

Let's say your friend got a promotion. You're genuinely happy for her. But something in your gut says, *When is it my turn?* You have an option. Stuff those feelings down or examine that feeling and ask, *What is this feeling?* It may be that it's time to examine what you really want. Maybe you need to voice a complaint to yourself about where you are and why it bothers you that you're there.

Sometimes women convince themselves they're happy without ever getting intentional about what they want, but in fact they're stuffing their feelings. We learned to stuff feelings as children. It's a strange thing, but it's true. Just think about when you were younger. When you cried in public, were you told to stop crying, or encouraged to express yourself? So many of us were told, "Don't be a baby" or "Stop that or I'll give you something to cry about." Very few of us were allowed or encouraged to express our true feelings or opinions as children. When faced with shame, the brain reacts as if it were facing physical danger and activates the sympathetic nervous system, generating the flight/fight/freeze response. The flight response triggers the feeling of needing to disappear, and children who have this response will try to become invisible.

It's hard to trust someone who covers up or won't admit the truth. If you're not being honest, you'll have trouble trusting yourself.

So it's no surprise that shame comes up when we admit our feelings.

Hear me: you are meant to feel it all. Emotions are part of the human experience. God made you this way for a reason! Feelings are feedback. By paying attention to your feelings and their feedback, you can identify what is unacceptable and unhelpful in your life. But only if you pay attention.

Acting like certain emotions aren't allowed makes Little You confused. She's got that lie detector, remember? She knows that you're not being honest about the reality of your life. It's hard to trust someone who covers up or won't admit the truth. If you're not being honest, you'll have trouble trusting yourself.

## Custom-Made Life

Nobody on the entire planet will answer "What's not working for me?" in the exact same way as you. It's a bespoke question—customized just for you! You have unique skills, talents, traits, and abilities. Your history isn't the same as anyone else's. And you face challenges nobody else faces in quite the same way.

Here it is again: What's not working *for me*? Don't miss that last part of the question. It's not, What's not working in the country or not working in my industry? This isn't a macro question. It's micro.

What might work just fine in someone else's life might not work for you. A certain level of success. A romantic life that's just so-so. Credit card debt. A sedentary lifestyle. Someone else might say, "That's fine," and accept things the way they are.

But not you. You want more. That's why you're here reading this book. You realize abundant life is already yours, it's just a matter of claiming it. More love. More joy. More impact. Making that vision a reality requires that you get super honest about where you currently are. Not what other people believe will work for you. Not what you see as part of the status quo.

What is not working *for you*?

Here's a glimpse of how this question worked for me recently.

I was experiencing conflict with a person on my team, and let me tell you: It. Was. Rough. I felt like I had extended help and kindness toward her. But I kept hearing that she gossiped and said ugly things about me behind my back. I was trying to build a better life, working toward my goals, but this conflict had me feeling stuck.

I wanted to ignore what was going on, and I for sure didn't want to dive into conflict. Dealing with her vibe was not something I looked forward to. But she was on my team. My goals were being thwarted by this recurring issue.

My complaint about this situation might seem obvious. My colleague was being mean. I didn't want her to be mean to me. I was the victim, and she was the aggressor. I wanted it to stop.

Simple, right?

Nope.

I took a deep breath and did a brain dump about what was not working for me in this situation. As I worked through the answer, layers emerged. I didn't like the feeling of being rejected by someone I was trying to be nice to. I didn't like the potential risk to my reputation. I kept thinking about the days when I was in school, the times when I wasn't popular, when I wasn't included. Those echoes from Little Me were finding their way into the story I was telling myself about my interaction with this person. It was all coloring what I was feeling. When I explored my complaint and got curious about it, the entire situation shifted.

The true answer to the question "What's not working for me?" was "I don't like feeling left out." It was more about my own fear of rejection than her behavior. And when I got honest, I realized her tendencies had to do with her own fears about her ability to juggle work and home and keep food on the table for her kids.

I began to speak truth to myself. I reminded myself that anyone who is doing great things and inspiring the world in a big way is not necessarily going to be liked by all.

It is safe to be me.

I like me.

Rejection is God's protection.

What could have been an unfortunate showdown ended up teaching me to extend grace and forgiveness—first to myself and then to this woman on my team.

Honestly answering "What's not working for me?" allowed me to get unstuck, move forward in our working relationship, and keep my own deeper needs from getting pulled into an unproductive tangle.

By answering "What's not working in my life?" you're taking back *your power.* When you feel safe and honestly explore your feelings, you can **voice** your complaint about what's going on in your life that isn't in alignment with who you are and want to be. That's a good thing.

In the next chapter, we'll **get curious** about your complaint and really dig in about what's not working and why. Explore with detachment. There is no need to worry or get bogged down—we're just exploring. We're going to discover some super valuable treasure there. Let's get into it!

**Your Turn**

## Crap Shoot

Give yourself permission to write down everything that's going on that you don't like. Get it out. Take off the gloves and just go at it. Unburden yourself by emptying your thoughts and emotions out in an intentional way. When we keep that stuff pushed down inside, it gets stuck. Getting radically honest about what's *not* working is essential to help you realize what you *really* want. Use the Freedom Wheel as a prompt:

- Health: _____

○ Wealth: _____

○ Career: _____

○ Spiritual Life: _____

○ Romantic Life: _____

○ Family Life: _____

- Social Life: _____

*Chapter Six*

# Get Curious

## *Question 2: When Did I First Start Accepting That?*

A wise man scales the city [walls] of the mighty
and brings down the stronghold in which they trust.

—PROVERBS 21:22

ONCE YOU'VE GOTTEN HONEST AND VOICED YOUR complaint, naming what's not working for you, it's time to get curious about why you've been settling for less than you deserve. Ask yourself the second question of Take 7: *When did I first start accepting that?* There was a moment in time when you believed and hoped for more. When did you stop? Likely it was a particular moment when that door closed for you. Your answer to question two may be immediately clear, or you may need to think about it awhile.

Journaling or getting to a new location can help. For me, getting outside is key. So grab a notebook and a pen or go for a walk outside to consider when you started accepting less than you deserve in this complaint. What doors have closed to you in the past? When did you quit hoping for more? What emotions come up for you?

## Messy Emotions

While emotions are endlessly fascinating to me, they can be messy. They can be inconvenient. We don't always want to deal with them. If we pay attention to our emotions, we sometimes discover we have work to do. Facing the truth of them can feel vulnerable and scary. I've had clients who say, "What if I start crying and I can't stop?"

All you need to do in this moment is get curious about what you feel. You are not your emotions—you have them; they don't have you. When you let yourself feel them and listen to what they're telling you, you'll be empowered.

Take my client Mina for example.

I still remember working with Mina on a particularly thorny problem. We'd gone outside to walk and talk. As the waves of the Pacific crashed on the shore, my bare feet made footprints alongside Mina's. We watched the tide rush up and wash them away. Taking my VIP coaching clients to the beach is one of my favorite ways to refresh our thinking. The tides remind us that

You are not your emotions—you have them; they don't have you. When you let yourself feel them and listen to what they're telling you, you'll be empowered.

life moves on, even when we're standing still. We get a whole new perspective. The vastness of the ocean reminds us how big God is. And the change of location makes space for reflection.

As we walked along the beach, Mina grew animated talking about how she'd started her own business, working from her kitchen table alongside a business partner. She believed so strongly in their shared mission. Customers' appreciation for their product made her feel a sense of purpose. She felt exhilarated by interacting with happy customers. Mina had enjoyed financial and emotional abundance through that business. It brought her a sense of purpose and joy.

But her relationship with her business partner wasn't as fruitful. Things soured between them. Their interactions became toxic. As a result, Mina pulled back from the business. She was still making a good monthly residual income without actively building the business, but she felt stuck. She missed the creativity and productivity of building something that mattered. She dreamed of going out on her own. She had an idea for creating her own product, but she was scared.

I asked Mina what was holding her back. She told me she worried her former partner was going to destroy her. The words tumbled out of her mouth:

*She will be so mad.*

*She'll be so disappointed.*

*I feel so guilty.*

*I feel like I owe her.*

Tears rolled down Mina's face as she shared how she didn't want to be in this working relationship anymore. But she worried her entire life would blow up in her face if she broke up the partnership. Mina was carrying heavy burdens. It was clear she felt super vulnerable, so I assured her she was safe. Nothing bad was going to happen. We were just exploring. It was okay that she was feeling some strong emotions. I was curious and wanted to encourage Mina to be curious too.

"When did you first start accepting that?" is not a test. It's an invitation to get curious. When noticing feelings like sadness, annoyance, anger, or disappointment, it's helpful to try to remember when you might have felt that way as a child.

Mina had been bracing for how her business associate might react to her choices, and she was afraid. I reminded her that how others feel is not our responsibility. We only control our actions. We cannot control how other people feel or act. Still, she insisted she felt responsible for how this woman would feel and act.

"When did you first start accepting that?" I asked.

As the wind blew and the waves crashed, Mina said, "My dad married my stepmom when I was ten. I tried to make her happy. I tried hard. But no matter what I did, she was never happy." Suddenly Mina saw the connection between her current stuck state and what her inner child was telling her.

That was huge. Mina recognized the moment when she'd started accepting less than she deserved.

Before she could move forward, that decades-old wound needed attention. Mina needed to process some feelings. How did she do it? She wrote two letters: one to her dad, saying, basically, *You brought somebody into my world who made me feel unsafe and made me start questioning myself. Here's how that made me feel.* As she wrote that letter, she gained a bunch of insights. She also wrote a letter to her stepmom that helped her process her emotions. Writing letters helped her process her feelings in a safe way. And by getting honest with herself about how the realities of life events shaped her character, she saw some blessings that came out of those hard situations. In the process, she even chose to forgive her dad, her stepmom, and herself.

After Mina got curious and discovered the moment on her timeline when she'd started accepting less than she deserved, she began to move forward with purpose. We continued to work through Take 7, and she had several breakthroughs to help her get to what she *really* wanted. (Spoiler: she ended up going out on her own to build her own product and built an incredibly successful business.)

When we don't voice our opinions or share an opposing view, it's often because we want to belong—we don't want to cause conflict. We can see conflict as a threat to our livelihood. So we shut down in the name of making everyone else happy and keeping the peace. Trying to meet other people's needs is not a solution. Meet your own needs first. That's why it's super important to answer for yourself, *When did I first start accepting this?*

## Wounded

When I'm coaching clients, father *and* mother wounds almost always come up. Even the most successful people have them. Children learn their worth from parents—not just from their parents' words but also from their actions. Sometimes a parent is absent, emotionally unavailable, or even hostile. If this happens in the relationship consistently or repeatedly, over time, a child's sense of worth can be significantly diminished. That wound might be obvious or hidden under the surface, quietly driving decisions on a subconscious level.

Maybe you connect with this experience and recognize that you have wounds of your own. You might say, *My parents did a great job—I don't think I have any wounds from them.* That may be true, but even the most loving and careful parents don't get it right 100 percent of the time. Even if your parents did a good job, you may have wounds. Both those things can be true at once.

If you feel any shame about admitting a mother or father wound—or both—please remember this: there is no condemnation in Christ Jesus (Romans 8:1). We all have wounds of some kind. Do not allow shame to stalk you. Block its number. You and shame don't belong in the same room.

My inner child started accepting the belief "I just need more money" when my mom started dating my stepdad. Up until that point she'd been able to pay her bills on time. She went to work and even worked on her days off, cutting hair inside our garage. My brother and I entertained ourselves by playing with our cousins or kids on the block. When my mom started dating my future stepdad, in her words, she started to "make bad decisions. We cared more about having fun on the weekends instead of paying the bills."

My mom didn't ever say, "We're poor." I just innately felt it. Then when our house went into foreclosure my suspicions were confirmed. That was when Little Me decided that if we just had more money, then my mom would be happy, my dad would be healthy, and we could all reunite as one big, happy family. Being poor and feeling shame were all tied up together somehow.

I carried a lot of shame in my life because I was embarrassed. I lied to hide the fact that my dad was in prison. I made up reasons that he wasn't around because I didn't want people to know. I felt even more shame when I lied, and I carried that with me. It felt heavy and empty. I was afraid. I was stuck.

When I was a teenager, I became the president of Friday Night Live, a community service club that worked to end binge drinking. I traveled all over California on that mission. Having substance abuse in my family background fueled me. And along the way I learned so much. I learned that my dad wasn't a bad person—he'd just made a bad choice. That bad choice led to another and to him becoming an addict. I also got involved in Al-Anon.

I began to deal with my shame. I stay attuned to my body for when shame comes up, and I'm quick to challenge it and bring it to light. I have a friend who says we need to shine a light in the closet to prove there's no bogeyman there. Once you shine a light on why you feel shame, you can be free.

## Get Curious About *You*

Take a deep breath—three breaths work well for me—and examine your feelings and thoughts. You may discover a wound that's been stealthily stealing your joy, robbing you of your vision, and blocking abundance in your life. Acknowledge the possibility that your scars may have healed over with scar tissue. Thanks to those scars, you're stronger as a person. More resilient.

Regardless of whether we have mother or father wounds, at some point we learn to settle for less than we deserve. Maybe you accepted the lie that growing up meant you'd never have the life

94

you wanted. That's why it's important to get curious here and stop letting unconscious beliefs drive your behavior.

Do you know the difference between a thermometer and a thermostat? A thermometer measures the temperature. My kitchen thermometer tells me if the turkey is fully cooked, and the one in the medicine cabinet can tell me if one of my kids has a fever. Thermometers give us information, but they don't have the power to change the temperature. They simply provide information.

A thermostat, however, is empowered to make a change. It monitors the temperature of the air and regulates it by blowing cold or hot air so that the room feels more comfortable. Have you ever set the thermostat to 62 degrees and later you suddenly realize that you're freezing? I have! The right thing to do is change the setting. Otherwise you'll just turn blue from the cold!

It's time to take your temperature (aka check your standard) and decide if that's still working for you. Why did you set your "thermostat" there to begin with? There was a reason you set that standard at that certain place. By asking yourself "When did I first start accepting that?" you'll recognize your ability to change that standard at any time.

## Nurture Your Inner Child

Nurture your inner child and speak truth to her—re-parent her. I'm not a therapist, but I've borrowed the word "re-parent" from therapy because, as a mom, I want to show Little Me the same kind of compassion and care I show my children. "Re-parenting" means offering Little Me the wisdom, love, and empowerment that experience has given me. It means listening with love and offering guidance. And when I say "re-parent," don't think I'm negating the parenting you already got. Thank God for the people who parented you—your parents, grandparents, guardians, whomever. They probably parented the way their parents did. We often repeat what we've seen modeled for us. This isn't about that.

Spend time with Little You. Nurture her the way you nurture the children in your own life—with love. Always speak to her kindly, helping her feel safe, and being gentle so she won't feel frightened, scared, or anxious. Remember that a hurting child needs comfort and reassurance. Parenting well means communicating unconditional love, then coaching as needed from a place of acceptance and wisdom.

Here's an example of what re-parenting my inner child looks like. Sometimes insecurity about my body pops up. For instance, I might be getting upset as I'm trying on clothes in a store. Little Me feared getting teased. I was called thunder thighs a lot by boys, and after that I never wanted to show my legs. The bullying and teasing hurt. Even now when I wear shorts, I often recall those words and I feel her pain.

When I sense that Little Me is feeling scared about teasing, I consciously choose to love myself unconditionally. I let her know that even if those statements were true once, that doesn't mean they apply now. I tell her what is most important to me—the grown-up me—and assure her that I will take care of her no

Parenting well means

communicating

unconditional love,

then coaching as

needed from a

place of acceptance

and wisdom.

matter what. (I'm proud to say that thirty years later, I can now wear shorts in public.)

You have a chance to choose what from the past you want to take with you into today and into the future. *You* get to choose. You determine what to keep and what to discard. No adult is wiser than you are anymore. *You* are the adult.

Now that you have **voiced** your complaint and **gotten curious** about why you've accepted less than you deserve, we're going to explore what it means to **nurture** yourself. This is a critical part of pursuing the life of your dreams—the life you were made for! In the next chapter we'll explore question 3: "What Little Me is showing up right now?"

Your Turn

## Dig In to Question 2

Think about your answer to "What's not working for me?" What in your life isn't working for you right now? Then get curious about why it's not working for you. Write down the reasons your life looks like it does. Start asking some clarifying questions:

- When did you start accepting this less-than-ideal situation?

- What was happening in your life at the time you started accepting it?

- Do the statements you tell yourself about this situation line up with the truths of Scripture and God's character?

- In what areas are you accepting less than abundance?

*Chapter Seven*

# Nurture Yourself

## Question 3: What Little Me Is Showing Up Right Now?

Just because things could, maybe, have been different
doesn't mean that things would have been better!

—DR. CAROLINE LEAF

THE STORIES WE TELL OURSELVES ABOUT OUR LIVES
don't emerge from a vacuum. Figuring out what is happening
in the background—what beliefs or assumptions are behind our
decisions—sheds light on all kinds of patterns on our thoughts
and choices.

Kids learn how to navigate the world from the patterns they
see around them. They unconsciously make up formulas like "if

X, then Y." For instance, "If families have enough money, they stay together. If families don't have enough money, they split up."

The rules from our childhood can follow us into adulthood. In adulthood we may be still subconsciously believing those rules and yet we're violating them. Confusion results. That confusion is Little You showing up, reminding you why you see life the way you do and where that information came from.

When we're unaware of the patterns and unconscious beliefs informing our lives, we can become stuck *or* we might jump ahead too quickly into frantic action, making matters worse. It's important to allow yourself to feel those feelings and examine the underlying belief driving your behaviors. It's time to remember. It's time to pay attention to Little You.

When I want to create change in my life, when I want to coach myself to the next level, I get curious about my timeline. I try to understand my own history. The Little Me that comes up when I meet resistance in my life thinks that I'm poor, even as my champion self sets huge business goals. If I don't meet those goals—even if I get 95 percent there—my first thought isn't my champion self asking, "Okay, what did you learn?" My first thought is, "Seriously, I needed more money than this!" I know, I know. Then I have to go through Take 7 *and* step into my champion self.

So get curious about your history. Become your own life's anthropologist. When you do, you'll start to see the whys behind your beliefs and what you're seeking. This can be so fun!

My client Joy is a great example of this. As I was working through Take 7 with her, Joy's curiosity kicked in big time on the "What Little Me is showing up right now?" question. She loved

When we're unaware

of the patterns and

unconscious beliefs

informing our lives,

we can become stuck

*or* we might jump

ahead too quickly into

frantic action, making

matters worse.

research, so she pulled a bunch of photos from storage and spread them all out on her kitchen table. Some had been displayed in frames in her family home for years; others hadn't been touched in decades. Now she peered at them like an archaeologist searching for clues, viewing them as if for the first time and asking herself, *When was each photograph taken? Where was I at the time? What was I doing? What was I thinking? What was I feeling?*

Joy created a timeline using these snapshots of her life and chose a few to share with me:

- The first is her at age three. Little Joy is reaching out to feel the mist of Niagara Falls from the railing, held safely in her mother's arms. Joy's family rarely traveled, so this had been an exotic trip for them. Her parents had borrowed a VW van, driving thousands of miles, for this adventure. They'd slept at campgrounds along the way where her dad was at ease while her mom fretted. Joy recalled her parents saying they could only persuade her to eat hot dogs or bacon on this trip. She's now been a vegetarian for decades.
- Here's Little Joy at age five, showing off a gap-toothed smile the day she lost her first tooth, sitting on the brick steps of her parent's tiny apartment. She'd just begun kindergarten in the same school where her dad taught. That was the year her baby brother was born, when she took on the role of Helpful Big Sister. She'd just learned to read—and worlds opened for her in a new way.
- Here's Joy in a fourth-grade yearbook photo taken at her new school, the year her parents bought the tiny home where they live to this day. She recalls how the other girls in

her class wore new outfits, their hair fixed just so. Joy wore a blue T-shirt and jeans, her hair in a messy ponytail. Her mom didn't keep up with the school calendar; she worked in an office and wasn't home much. Joy's too-big smile masks unease. Though she felt like she didn't fit in, she fake-smiled through her pain.

- At age fifteen, here's Joy at journalism camp, editor of the school newspaper. In this photo she's eating pizza with other campers, far from the gravity of her parents' rules and her hometown classmates' expectations, exploring her talents and gifts.

- Here's Joy at age twenty. She's at a college sorority luau wearing a lei, her smile wide and genuine. She recalls making friends beyond her tiny hometown and how her dreams for the future were coming into focus.

- Next is a blurry photo of twenty-three-year-old Joy holding a store-bought daisy bouquet and wearing a floral dress. The photo was taken on the porch of her family friend's home—a wedding venue her friend had accepted but didn't really want.

- The next photo is Joy at age twenty-five, leaning forward to pick up her firstborn on the playground of his nursery school. She's smiling, but her body is too thin after months of breastfeeding, childrearing, and launching her own business. Closer inspection reveals a cold sore on her lip. Were she and her husband merely experiencing newlywed woes or had Joy made a terribly wrong choice?

- At age thirty-five, this photo of Joy shows her with eyes half closed, visibly exhausted and holding one young child while flanked by two more, giggling in pajamas. That was the year her boss offered her a promotion and she'd laughed out loud. She didn't believe she could handle more than she was already juggling.

- Here's Joy at age forty-four, leaning in to answer a question on a panel at an industry event. She'd just left her corporate job to start a new company. With a divorce behind her, she looks lighter, brighter, and more comfortable in her own skin.

I sensed Joy's compassion and pride for the younger Joy in those photos. I know how looking at them felt. "I feel love for her," she said. "She's been through a lot."

Going through her photos this way helped Joy see a pattern. Her fear of being rejected was at the root of her settling for less than she deserved. It started when she moved to a new town at ten and it became a survival skill. Was that skill still serving her well now? If not, what could she do differently?

Once she clearly understood this wound of fearing rejection, Joy was able to *nurture* her inner child. Joy gave Little Joy attention and love, showing her evidence of the courage illustrated in the photos she'd seen. Her complaint was still there, but she was beginning to see her situation in a new light.

## Creating Your Timeline

Now it's your turn. Take time to recall random memories and past versions of you. Think about what was happening in those memories. This is an important step in learning to nurture Little You. That's what a timeline is for.

Thinking through your timeline can take many forms. To get you started, here are a few ways that my clients and I have seen success in creating a timeline.

- **Journaling.** Journaling can be a great way to begin. This is about getting your thoughts and feelings out on paper. Throw caution to the wind. Do not edit yourself and don't worry about complete sentences or punctuation—or what someone might say if they ever read the words on the page. Handwriting doesn't count today. You can even type it on your phone or laptop if you want. The point is to get it out there.

- **Interviewing.** Asking friends and family about their memories of you can also help you to gain insight about Little You. This has been especially helpful to those of my clients who have trouble tapping into childhood memories. Siblings, childhood friends, and other family members may help call up memories long forgotten. The caution here is that other people's memories of you are incomplete. They're remembering from their unique perspective, too, so take what they say with a grain of salt.

- **Reviewing Photos.** Like Joy, I like to look at old photos to connect with Little Me. I keep a box of them in my office so that when I get stuck, I can pull them out and remember some of the things Little Me has been through and accomplished. It's a great way to connect with myself.

Here I'd ask you to RUC: Resist the Urge to Criticize. Some of us have the habit of critiquing the appearance of ourselves or others. When we critique the past versions of ourselves, we're missing out on what we could see. We miss the takeaways gained through seeing the true story revealed in a picture. We might miss the expression or the body language or the interaction between the people featured. Let's try to see as a loving parent or, better yet, as God sees.

When it comes to creating a timeline, there's no right or wrong way to do it. Figure out what works for you; only *you* can do this work. You're the only person on the planet who can investigate your experiences. Even if you had a sibling—a twin for example— who was with you in every single waking moment of your life so far, the two of you would experience those moments differently. That's what's so amazing to me. It's up to *you* to be honest about your unique memories in your timeline. As you reflect on your past, patterns will begin to emerge.

If for some reason you feel blocked while doing the timeline exercise, examine the following:

- What are your fears around going through your timeline?
- What are the good things that might come of it?
- What would life look like if you did it?
- What are some tangible outcomes if you feel the feelings?

Show your mind proof that something *better* is on the other side of this work. By curiously examining your own timeline, you can identify which earlier version of you may have grabbed the wheel in the drive of life you're currently navigating. It could be the best thing you can do in this present moment to acknowledge and even celebrate her.

# Timeline Exercise

- **Look at your life in increments.** You can zoom in more closely as you feel inclined. Initially you might think, *I can't remember anything.* That's okay. It's because you're blocked on that for some reason. If you don't have anything, no biggie—move on. There is no right answer here. No judgment. Give yourself freedom to recall what's important to you right now.
  - Start with birth to age five. Do you know your birth story?

    What's the first story that comes to mind when you think about
  - ages 6–10,
  - ages 11–13,
  - ages 14–17,
  - ages 18–24, and
  - ages 25–30?

    Then take it by decades. The thirties. Forties. And so forth.
- **Consider the significant memories from those times.** Pay attention to any messages, motivations, hiccups, truths, and lies that arise in your memory. By looking at life in increments, you'll be giving yourself space and grace to make associations as needed.

- **Give Little You a chance to get caught up on the changes in your life.** For instance, maybe you've had daddy issues. Now you're in a relationship with a completely safe person. He has every characteristic you want in a good man. But your inner child isn't up to speed. She's not sure it's safe to be with a man. So she pops up with feelings of guilt and shame around intimacy and sex.

   Now you can get super honest with Little You. Show her evidence that you're in a safe relationship. Talk to her about what's important to you. It's not about judging or criticizing anything in your past, it's about learning and growing. Again, curiosity shapes this process. Leaning in to notice with love and compassion will help you identify truths.

I love that this exercise lets you both think about where you've been and celebrate different parts of you. You can be more connected and more powerful. It's time for paying tribute and celebrating. You're going to smile a lot, I think.

Right now, think about Little You. Ponder the influence she has on your today. She's there, to be sure, and her voice matters. As sure as you're physically and spiritually present in this moment, you are also carrying the voice of your eight-year-old self, your twenty-two-year-old self, and all the past versions of you deep inside. Say to yourself, "Whatever you need, it's okay. We can figure this out."

Choose to spend time with Little You. You can do this any way you like. It can be sitting quietly with her. Maybe go for a walk. Even find a swing and swing for a bit. Speak validation to her. Check in on the part of you that's upset. Ask, *What's the background on why this bothers me?* Let her know, *I see you. I love you. You're safe. Everything will be okay.*

Only you can parent her through the moment you're in. In the beginning re-parenting yourself may feel a bit odd. But there's nothing more natural in the world than tending to Little You.

Do you have to do this assignment? No. You don't have to do it. But if you resist creating a timeline, you'll never know the huge difference it might make. You'll wonder, *What would be different if I had done it?* It's like I say when I'm about to do a workout: persist through it and get to it! You'll be glad you did.

Whatever you choose, allow yourself to respond with compassion to the younger versions of you. We don't spend enough time loving every part of ourselves. We spend a lot of time being mad and criticizing ourselves. If you want others to love you well, first love yourself well.

## Box of Reminders

The other day I was feeling stressed about a situation with my daughter. I pulled out some old photos of me and a Polaroid stopped me in my tracks. It was taken when I was fourteen on a mission trip in Costa Rica. That version of Little Me was so fired up. My faith burned white hot. I would go around and pray over people. I prayed for revival every single day. That version of me was so committed. I wanted to change the world and make it a better place.

When I learned about this mission trip, I knew my family couldn't afford to pay for me to go. It cost $3,500. To me that was so much money. I didn't know if I could earn enough. But I sold sugar scrubs and bath salts to raise the funds. I worked so hard to raise that money—and I did it! When I got to go on the trip, I was elated. It was my dream come true.

I love this version of Cayla. She was so optimistic and hopeful. I tend to be critical of myself, but when I recall that struggle and that win, I feel proud. I can acknowledge the difficulty of that situation and admire how strong and tenacious that Little Me was in the face of those challenges. She had such clarity of purpose. I recognize that's a trait I show to this day.

Another thing I feel when I see that Polaroid is compassion. That version of Little Me got angry and confused when people wouldn't or couldn't support her going on that mission. She hadn't learned yet that not everyone wants to help. Or that even admirable goals won't always be shared.

I had some major trust and control issues for a lot of years, specifically with men. I did not feel safe, so I tried to control others with anger. In my career as a nurse, I'd felt intimidated by the male doctors. I dealt with those feelings by being dominating and controlling. That worked in some ways because it led to my being promoted to charge nurse. But my behavior wasn't in alignment with who I am at my core. It was a survival mechanism.

Subconsciously I believed my options were to either be weak or to dominate everybody. There was no way I would allow myself to be weak again as I believed I'd been as a child, so I dominated. It didn't feel good to me because my true nature isn't to be dominating or putting people in their places. That was me acting out of Little Me's fear. The beliefs and behaviors that helped me survive weren't working for me anymore. Something didn't feel right. Something was off.

Once I figured out what was driving my dominating behavior and I connected the dots, I knew that growth, for me, would come from a place of forgiveness. So I did the work. I worked through my feelings, thoughts, and behaviors and came to a place of genuine forgiveness. I got rid of the hate and came to a place of compassion. When I did that, my defensive behavior was no longer necessary. The poison was out of my body. It was so freeing! The person I am at my core came into alignment with my behavior. I brought Little Me in on the celebration. I said, "Look, we're good now. We're safe. And we're over it." I spoke kindly to her, took her to the passenger seat, and then let my champion self drive.

## Constant God

If you're a little blown away remembering how much change you've already encountered in your life, if you're intimidated or

Once I figured out
what was driving my
dominating behavior
and I connected the
dots, I knew that
growth, for me, would
come from a place
of forgiveness.

anxious as you anticipate change, you're not alone. Change is stressful. It can be scary. But I've got good news.

God does not change. Unlike us, God is permanent. The One who created the earth, stars, sky, and everything in this world knows *you*. He knows every thought in your head (and every hair on it!). God is the same yesterday, today, and forever (Hebrews 13:8). Always good, always kind, always loving, always merciful, always just. And there for you.

That will not change.

It can feel like this crazy world moves faster than we'd like, but our God never moves. Plant your feet on that solid Rock. It even helps to put your feet firmly under your body as you speak that truth aloud: "God is my rock." When you have a steady foundation and are clear on what you stand for and what you believe in and what's important to you, you become unshakable.

Is there a prayer you can lift up for Little You? Sometimes we get so used to the idea of prayer that we forget how big the idea is. It's a request to the God of the universe. God isn't subject to time limits as we are! The same God who cares for the sparrow and the wildflowers knows your every thought and numbers your steps. Ask God to step into the moment you're in *with you*. Remember, he is completely unbound by time. He invites you to ask for help. What's your prayer?

Once you've **voiced** your complaint, **gotten curious** about when you started accepting less than you deserve, and **nurtured** Little You, you're ready for question 4: "What is a better way of looking at this?"

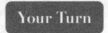

## Nurturing Little You

To nurture Little You, try using your senses.

- **See.** I'm a visual learner, so visual cues stimulate my imagination. If you're like me, create a chat book, box, or bowl of photos of you from the past.
- **Hear.** Auditory learners often find listening to music from earlier eras in their lives works best.
- **Touch.** If you're more tactile and touch helps engage your imagination, find an object like a soft blanket, a toy, a puzzle, a book, or a stuffed animal. I've found that a trip to a toy store works well to help women connect with their inner child.
- **Smell.** Scents are fabulous for memory connections. Even the words "cinnamon," "vanilla," "lemon," or "mint" are likely to trigger your own memories of something from childhood. Try focusing on smells and seeing what memories those scents bring up.
- **Taste.** Drinking or eating something nostalgic can also be a great option.

It doesn't matter which of your senses you engage so long as you are intentional about connecting with Little You, engaging your body in the process.

*Chapter Eight*

# Reframe It

## Question 4: What Is a Better Way of Looking at This?

> The real voyage of discovery consists not in seeking new lands but in seeing with new eyes.
>
> —MARCEL PROUST

ONCE YOU'VE SPENT TIME WITH YOURSELF, NUR-turing Little You in response to what triggered your complaint, the next question prompts you to reframe and asks, *What is a better way of looking at this?* It's a lot like climbing up from the beach to the clifftop.

## Perspective

I love the ocean. When I'm gazing out at that great expanse of blue-green water, I can lose track of time. The water looks so

117

smooth out there. Walking on the beach I watch the waves build, gather. Foam bubbles up, forming white caps. As the waves rush to shore, the white caps dissolve into patches of tiny bubbles. Those bubbles pop, dissolving into seawater that rushes back, returning to the great expanse of ocean.

Going up on the cliff gives me a totally different perspective than when I'm sinking my toes into the sand. Up high, I can't see those little bubbles. Instead, I can see way out to sea. I might glimpse a whale, or a bunch of dolphins, or watch as a ship sails off beyond the horizon. Perspective matters. Sometimes you need to pull back. Other times you need to zoom in. Perspective requires a shift. A reframe.

With question 1 you voiced your pain point. With question 2 you got curious about when you started accepting that pain. With question 3 you nurtured that Little You. Now you can go from suffering to rising. The way you do that is by shifting your perspective. You'll move from seeing something as a problem to viewing it as a challenge. There's a huge reframe.

See, by definition, a problem is an unpleasant or harmful thing. It's something to be dealt with or overcome. A challenge, on the other hand, is a call to engage—an opportunity, so to speak. A flat tire is a problem. A dance-off is a challenge. A burnt casserole is a problem. A bake-off is a challenge.

## Blocked by Anger

"What if I'm not ready to reframe?"

That question pops up a lot. And it's totally normal. If that's your response, my question back to you is, "What are you angry

Maybe you don't know. You're not even sure what you

about?" Maybe you don't know. You're not even sure what you feel. You're locked up inside.

Let me introduce you to a life-changing exercise called anger release.

Candidly, when I first learned about anger release, I resisted it. Intellectually it made sense to me but my spirit resisted it. I was working with a coach who took me through the process over the phone and, let me tell you, I felt so dumb. I gave it a half effort. I couldn't get into it.

But the idea stayed with me. I knew I had unexpressed anger. That energy felt bottled up inside me. For whatever reasons—a million reasons, maybe—I had kept the anger inside. And I could taste the bitterness. So later, alone, I gave anger release a try. Without my coach on the other end of the phone, I felt more comfortable letting loose.

It. Was. Amazing.

I got all my anger out in a couple of minutes—three minutes at the most. I felt so much better, so much lighter—like I'd lost a hundred pounds. I thought, *Why have I been resisting this?* Anticipating the anger felt worse than feeling it and letting it out.

This was good news.

## The Transforming Power of Anger Release

The first time I did the exercise, I went inside a closet and locked the door. I told Chase to take the kids out for a while. I started punching a pillow and screaming. I didn't even know what I was mad about—there were years of anger built up. I just screamed and punched. It was cathartic.

# Anger Release Exercise

Simply put, anger release is acknowledging the feelings that are stuck inside you. It's about expressing them. Releasing them. It's a way to let that energy move out of the body. It's simple but effective. I'll walk you through it right now.

1. Just close your eyes. Take a deep breath. I put both hands over my heart at first. It helps you to ground yourself and feel safe.
2. Keep taking deep breaths. Every time you exhale, fill in the blank: "I am angry because _____" or "I'm angry about _____." Answer out loud. Or write it on paper, type it on your phone—whatever works for you. Don't filter. Just let the words come.
3. Anger is energy. You want to get that energy out. Punch a pillow, stomp your feet, shake your body, scream, or yell into a pillow if that's what you need to do. Give yourself a physical outlet to let that release out in a natural way.

Little You needs to say things. Things that were ignored or never heard. Emotions from moments when she wasn't protected or nurtured. Let her voice those things. Let her be angry. Whatever she's feeling is okay. Let her know it's okay to let it all out. She's safe now.

You will be amazed at how much better you'll feel when you acknowledge and release the anger you've kept inside. And you'll wonder why you waited so long.

Now if I know I'm mad about something, I give myself permission to get it out as quickly as I can. I release that negative energy out of my body.

Little kids having a temper tantrum do this naturally. Sometimes when we go to our inner child, she'll need to rant and rave. To cry. As it says in Ecclesiastes 3, there's a time to mourn, a time to grieve—a time for everything. A time for processing the bad circumstances Little You endured. A time to be ticked off.

Now I go to my rage room to release my anger. Okay, it's just my closet, but it works nicely for rage. In the privacy of my closet, I let my anger out in two or three minutes. Just throwing a little fit if I need to. After that I can move on without baggage. The anger moves through me quickly these days now that I've had practice with letting it out instead of trying to stuff it down. I can let go of it pretty much anyplace that's safe and private. My car works. The shower works too.

So many of us women have been trained to push our anger down and never show it. There's this stigma around angry women that makes us feel shame for even *feeling* anger, much less expressing it. It's so unhealthy to heap shame on top of anger when anger is not a sin—it's simply an emotion that we are 100 percent allowed to feel.

At our Mommy Millionaire retreats we coach women on how to release anger, and I've seen incredible results with this. We've provided them with a safe place specifically set aside for anger release. We supply boxing gloves, punching bags, pillows—all the things. The freedom I've seen women experience as a result is incredible.

I'll never forget this one transformative anger release that happened with a woman named Kathy. She'd expressed her goal of becoming a coach. I had seen that she was committed to the training, but at the retreat weekend she seemed detached. Unengaged. Like a ghost. I was having a hard time wrapping my head around her in a coaching role. She just seemed so flat. I knew she had the wisdom and knowledge to share and a desire inside to help women, but her outsides didn't match her insides.

Imagine my surprise when I saw Kathy in the anger release room. She'd been stone-faced moments before, but now she was shouting, punching, yelling. She went hard at it for five or six minutes. Kathy had weathered some difficult things in her marriage some years ago, and though she and her husband had successfully navigated those challenges and been happily married since, she'd bottled up her anger and never released it. After the anger release, she was like a child after a temper tantrum—spent. Exhausted.

The transformation was immediate. Kathy started to engage with the rest of us in a genuine, caring way. There was a joy about her I hadn't seen before. It was incredible. The barrier that had kept her from being fully present was gone. Poof. Nothing externally had changed for her, but something inside her had shifted. She'd made space for something beautiful to grow inside where that anger had been taking up space.

What if you let go of the knot of anger that you've been carrying around? Holding on to it poisons you from the inside. Once you let go, you'll be reluctant to live with anger eating you up inside again.

## After the Anger

Expressing anger is liberating because anger and bitterness cloud our imagination and our vision. When that anger is gone, you're freed from distractions. Free to see clearly. Free to change your perspective. Free to find your purpose.

When anger isn't crowding our emotional space, we have room for the passion and compassion we're created to enjoy. By feeling and releasing the anger, we have a new perspective. We can reframe. We gain clarity. Clarity makes way for creative thinking.

When Rachel and I first met, she'd decided she was ready for a change. She owned a successful credit card processing business, but having achieved many of her goals, she identified a complaint—she was no longer enjoying her day-to-day work life. She wanted to do something more with her life. So she was preparing to sell her profitable business to chase something that might give her that longed-for sense of purpose. She wasn't sure what that would be yet.

As we began working through Take 7, she began to reframe her current situation. She discovered that helping her employees grow through one-on-one coaching and mentoring absolutely lit her up. She loved the "helping high"—the natural cocktail of oxytocin, serotonin, and dopamine that comes with helping others. (Not only does it make you feel good and boost your mood, it also counteracts the effects of the stress hormone cortisol.) Rachel found her purpose *inside* her existing business.

## Switching Things Up with Perspective

Our lives are a story we tell. You may have told a part of your story so many times—maybe even when trying to resolve a conflict

Living your best

life, living out your

testimony, is why

you're here.

with friends or family—that you no longer perceive it accurately. Many people are stuck in a limited perspective of their story. Stay stuck or move forward. The choice is yours.

Living your best life, living out your testimony, is why you're here. This is your temporary home. Your eternity in heaven is secure. Live with that end in mind, keeping your eye on the prize: hearing that "Well done!" That's going to happen by accepting what's been given to you and allowing God to use that for good in your life.

I don't want you to miss out on the value in your situation because of your perspective. So let's try some new ways of seeing, shall we?

## THE GOLDEN TICKET

My daughter Charlie loves acting. I got to see her perform as Willy Wonka in the musical version of *Willy Wonka and the Chocolate Factory*. It was surreal to see her in a story about a poor kid whose family has almost no resources—sound familiar? In the play, the character named Charlie (along with a few other kids who received a golden ticket) gets to come with the mysterious Willy Wonka on a tour of his magical factory. What's beautiful is that Charlie's life experiences uniquely equipped him for the special role of inheriting the factory. Though the other children want it, they haven't had the hard life experiences that Charlie has that makes him able to appreciate it the way he does.

Try thinking of the challenge you're currently in as your golden ticket. You're in the moment where you're about to come into the opportunity of a lifetime. What inheritance might your life have prepared you for? You're a child of God and he has something good for you—abundance, joy, peace, and so much more. What does God have in store for you because of your current situation?

I love Willy Wonka's emphasis on imagination. We've gotten good at training our minds to see what's not good, what's less-than. How many critical thoughts a day do we have? Too many! But worrying depletes energy. Try accessing your childlike imagination and engaging it to notice all the things going right, all the things that are possible, all the things that have—imagine that—gone well! The hot running water in the shower, the ice in your freezer, the electricity running into your house—all the small wonders we take for granted. Nurture that childlike faith in all the abundance already coming to you. When you start noticing, it can be amazing! Start to imagine: "How cool will it be when things work out?"

## S'MORES ANYONE?

Shame and blame. Those evil twins are the enemies of creativity. They are the enemies of freedom.

If you're ready to be rid of the shame and blame you've been carrying around, light it up! Light an actual fire in a fireplace, a grill, or an outdoor fire pit. Write down words about the shame and blame you've been carrying and then set fire to the paper. Let 'em burn! You weren't meant to carry those accusations around. Even visualizing setting those false burdens on fire can be powerful.

God is ready to exchange your ashes for beauty. As you bravely toss your shame and blame on the flames, what beautiful things arise from those ashes?

## THE TRAFFIC JAM

My friend recently taught me a trick. When she gets stuck in a traffic jam or delay, she says aloud, "Whew! What a relief." Even if she's in a hurry. That verbal cue is her way of reminding herself she's not the one waiting on the side of the road for the tow truck—or an ambulance.

Say aloud, "Whew! That worked out well for me!" Those words remind your brain that the challenge you're facing is uncomfortable, but you have been spared something worse. How will you use the time and space you're in now to help yourself and others?

## THE FLIP

Your creativity may be blocked by the constancy of your environment. Try physically changing your location to clear your head and create space for creativity. Changing your location has been shown to stimulate creativity.[1]

Try going to someplace new or sitting in an unusual way—say cross-legged on the floor in the grass. Or stand up and dance in your living room or office! Once you've switched things up, allow yourself space to imagine your current challenge. Ask, *Is there a different way for me to see this?*

## MEETING WITH YOUR BIOGRAPHER

There's something fascinating to me about reading biographies and interviews with people who've achieved big things. It's one reason I love doing my podcast![2] I love learning about what makes people tick and how they got to where they are now.

What might journalists or historians or your biographer say about your current challenge twenty years from now? Will this

God is ready to

exchange your ashes for

beauty. As you bravely

toss your shame and

blame on the flames,

what beautiful things

arise from those ashes?

challenge have been a turning point for you? How? Or will it be a blip that doesn't register?

## OPTICAL ILLUSIONS

Instead of thinking about your challenge specifically, find something else to fix your focus on. One friend works on puzzles when she needs to give her brain a rest from a perplexing problem. Another does crossword puzzles. Another takes walks, noticing all the flora and fauna around her neighborhood.

Focusing on something with lots of details and pieces frees up our unconscious to solve problems for us. Maybe there's a piece you've been searching for that's been hiding from you in plain sight.

## BEAUTY BOOTCAMP

How strange it must've been for Esther in the Bible to be away from her family for months, getting beauty treatments alongside the other "bachelorettes" on the off chance that she might be chosen as the queen for the king. When she was chosen, she probably had a serious case of imposter syndrome. What I love best about Esther's story is how she realized that her strange timeline was all "for such a time as this" (Esther 4:14). Her time of preparation led to her stepping up boldly to speak up for a whole race of people who would've otherwise been wiped out. And because of her, the line of David was preserved, making way for Jesus to come into the world. Can you imagine? Now *that's* some reframing of perspective right there!

Maybe you're in a season of preparing now for your own "such a time as this."

## This Happened *for* You, Not *to* You

It's a big mind shift to go from seeing the events of your life as happening *to* you to understanding that they're happening *for* you. You're in this place for a reason—for your good and for the good of others. That's empowering! Even undeniably bad things can be reframed as setting you up for being your champion self.

For example, I hated my dad's addiction issues because they created all sorts of problems for him that made him effectively absent when I was growing up. There are times to this day that I feel anger around that issue. When I feel upset again, instead of seeing it as a *setback*, I recall that God used my history as a *setup*. He set me up to be an achiever for my family and to be a motivator for women, like my mom, to have financial empowerment. My history set me up to marry a husband of strong character who puts family first. And it set me up to give back to people who struggle as we did, especially in prison ministries, showing kids that they don't have to be victim to their parents' choices.

You've let your emotions about your circumstances flow out of you. Now turn your attention to how those circumstances can grow and strengthen you, preparing for a divine plan already in motion.

Stop struggling against who you're not and what you don't want. Hold open hands. Let go and release that stuff. Your purpose is way bigger than you can imagine. Lean into who you're designed to be. Lean into what matters.

Take a few minutes to think about the complaint you **voiced**—
your answer to the question "What's not working for me?" You
**got curious** about which Little You was showing up when you
felt that way, and you **nurtured** that Little You. Now that you've
**reframed** your perspective, you're ready for the next question:
"Where is there space for gratitude in this?"

WHAT DO YOU *REALLY* WANT?

Your Turn

## Climb Up

It's time to leave the beach and climb up to a higher place to get a new perspective on where you've been. The very things that light you up were placed inside you on purpose. You were meant to be you—happy, healthy, peaceful, living in abundance. You are God's masterpiece created to do good works.

- **Take a deep breath.** Then take two more.
- **Assess where you are in your body, mind, and spirit.** Get comfortable. Be reminded of the peace available to you by virtue of Jesus' promise. You're safe.
- **Imagine that you're rising above your sitting body.** Your essence, your soul, rises like a bird, rising to the top of the building you're in, up through the roof, up, up, and into the sky, up with the clouds.

    You can see what's below and you can also see what's happened before this moment on the timeline. You're looking back in time, to your timeline and all the versions of Little You. You love all those versions of yourself. Little You is doing the best she can in that moment.

- **See yourself in a moment on your timeline when you didn't like how it felt.** It's uncomfortable for you down there, but up here where you are right now, you have perspective. You have access. No judgment. Just compassion and perception.
- **What does your future look like?** From up high, in the timeline of your life you can see what's gone before and what's to

132

come. How is Little You doing? Does seeing the future you make you smile?

- **What are possible outcomes from this current moment of discomfort?** Take time to journal or talk about the positive potential in this challenge.
  - Write out your situation or complaint. (Use the Freedom Wheel if you need a prompt.)
  - What good might come from this situation in a best-case scenario? (For example, wisdom, experience, connection, financial good, career change, health improvement, or relational connections.)
  - How might this work out for your good and God's glory?
- **How are you feeling?** If you feel yourself triggered, you're going to your amygdala, which doesn't have a time stamp. To your emotions, a remembered traumatic event of the past may as well be happening now, which is why it may feel so intense. The amygdala is a primitive and aggressive part of the brain, so we want to bring you back to a more rational state. Ask these four questions to identify and then defuse emotion, while also helping yourself get helped:

  - What am I feeling?
  - When have I felt this way before?
  - What did I need in that moment? (It may be as simple as needing a hug or hearing "it's okay.")
  - How can I get that right now?

  Whether that's a hug from a loved one or hugging yourself, it will be soothing. However, the answer to what you need cannot be "I need *them* to _____." This is about what *you* need, not about what needs to change about another person's behavior. (For example, "I need him to stop working so much" may need to be stated as "I need to be reminded that I'm desired, I'm valuable and enjoyable to be around, and I need to lovingly share my needs with him.")

After you've worked through those emotions and soothed Little You, you'll be able to pull back and see your situation in a fresh way. You'll have reframed it!

*Chapter Nine*

# Be Thankful

*Question 5: Where Is There Space
for Gratitude in This?*

Gratitude makes sense of our past, brings peace
for today, and creates a vision for tomorrow.

—MELODY BEATTIE

YOU'VE BEEN TAKING STOCK OF YOUR TIMELINE
and you've reframed to see what gifts those times in your life gave
you—gifts of character, connection, or resources.

Question 5 invites you to offer thanks so you can feel authentic joy. When you get intentional with your gratitude, amazing
fruits will grow in your life:

- You'll gain *insight* into what matters to you.
- You'll recognize your own *agency.*
- You'll be empowered to change your situation and get
  *good results.*

Here's a quick story to illustrate how gratitude yields insight, agency, and good results. Not long ago I paid a significant sum to a company for a marketing service. After several months it became clear that they were not going to deliver on their promises. I was shocked. The level of deception this company went to was unsettling. My team encouraged me to take this company to court. I seriously considered it.

After praying about it, I realized that if I live my life looking in a rearview mirror, I will never get to my destination. Driving that way will get you nowhere—unless you mean to drive into a brick wall. Instead, I decided to work through Take 7.

- **What's not working for me in my life?** This company has my money and they're not acting with integrity.
- **When did I first start accepting that?** I started accepting less than excellent behavior when I was a child, especially from men.
- **What Little Me is showing up right now?** Fourteen-year-old Cayla who just wants to fit in. She wants everyone to like her.
- **What's a better way of looking at this?** This experience taught me to notice red flags. From now on, I'll always do my due diligence and get multiple quotes before signing a contract with a vendor.

- **Where is there space for gratitude?** The disappointment I had in this company made me appreciate the people and companies I love working with. I got curious about the attributes that make me want to work with them more. I made a list of those values—for instance, excellence, integrity, faith, and teamwork. I felt genuine gratitude for the circumstances and the people who'd been a part of my life, especially those that embodied those values—it was like a light turned on in my mind.

  Those characteristics I was listing perfectly described Donna, a woman who'd taken my Money Mentality programs. I hadn't connected with her in some time, but I realized I wanted her on our team. I didn't hesitate at all. I reached out to her and asked if she'd be interested in joining our team. We talked for a while about what her needs were and what my needs were, and we found a perfect fit.

The benefits of gratitude have been written about at length elsewhere. But what may surprise you is the mind shift that happens when you express gratitude when people do not seem to be a blessing at all. They seem like sources of pain or grief. They seem like obstacles to your success.

But once I'd voiced my frustration, got curious about where it was coming from, nurtured my inner child, then reframed the situation and thanked God for what he'd already done, I received the amazing gift of the right connection at the right time. As usual, God knew what I needed before I did. *And* he knew what Donna needed.

How is this

happening

for me and

not to me?

## Gratitude Is a Choice

Gratitude is a choice. It's the choice that takes you into a better tomorrow.

Take Christina for example. She wanted to be a movie star. She came to Hollywood when she was twenty and worked hard at it. She got a lot of supporting roles, but time after time, the leading role went to somebody else. Rejection after rejection toughened her skin. She kept working at the craft and learned not to take no for an answer. After she'd worked for ten years at it, she tried out for a part she really wanted—and didn't get it. She told me she felt like a loser.

That's when she voiced her complaint: her dream wasn't working for her anymore. She was sad. She got curious. When she thought about her inner child, she realized Little Christina hadn't gotten the attention she craved. When she spent time with her to nurture her, Christina realized she had the attention she needed. She had good friends and family in her life who loved her well. So then she was able to put Little Christina into a seat on the bus instead of letting her be in the driver's seat. She reframed her situation, asking, *How is this happening for me and not to me?*

Christina's journey had prepared her for her future. She took stock of what she'd learned from her acting pursuit: She knew how to make a good impression. She'd learned to promote and to sell. She'd gotten great at performing. She'd learned all sorts of media techniques. She'd developed a wonderful network. And she'd gotten rejected so much that she was hardly fazed by rejection—she'd developed thick skin. That was something not a lot of people can say. And Christina realized that when she started out as an actress, she absolutely did not have thick skin. She was tender and craved approval. Her acting career had trained that out of her.

She was super grateful for those things and saw that she wanted to advocate for other actors. She could take all those skills and create a publicity company. And she did! She moved into something way better and now she helps so many people—including herself.

While gratitude is a choice, that doesn't mean it's an easy choice to make. If you want to go after the life you really want, make the choice toward gratitude. Just like Christina, you are a champion. You are someone who can win in life. You can experience significant victory and opportunity and prosperity. You get to make decisions based on your champion self. Working through Take 7 means you're choosing to show up as a champion. You can choose to operate from abundance instead of from a scarcity mindset.

## Gratitude + Compassion

You choose how you show up in the world. That's a huge thing to be thankful for! While you're in this place of gratitude, don't forget to have compassion. Nurture yourself.

Christina did that when she acknowledged all the years of rejection and the misery of barely getting by—lots of doors slammed in her face. There was lots of sadness and hurt. She chose to be grateful for that version of herself that kept persisting in the dream and not giving up. And to be grateful for the moment when she said, "Hey, this isn't working for me anymore."

The hurts and struggles shaped her. Because of what she'd been through, Christina was able to turn that into something powerful. She's much happier today. And that's something to be extremely proud of and grateful for.

One more word about Christina. To this day Christina is quick to thank the people she'd surrounded herself with when she was chasing her acting dreams. She'd met and cultivated relationships in the publicity world. How else could she have realized she had the skills and desire to do that? As you go through Take 7, keep that in mind. As you're stepping into who you're meant to be, it's so important who you surround yourself with. Choose people who help expand your life and not shrink it.

Look for expanders, not shrinkers.

The most successful people practice extravagant gratitude. I've seen it so often, and I've experienced it so much myself that I believe it's a universal truth. The most grateful people—those who look for a way to say thanks in all circumstances—have cracked the code. That decision changes the trajectory of their lives. They are happier. They are fearless about who they want to be.

I've experienced the tremendous power of thanks. I know and believe you can have that power too.

A few years ago I got power back in my own life through gratitude. When my stepdad left my mom with nothing after almost twenty years together, it stopped me in my tracks. My whole world felt upside down. I never saw it coming. I was eight months pregnant with my second child, trying to run my own business, and suddenly there I was also taking care of my mom. I love my mom so much, and I felt very angry seeing her in pain. It had all the feelings. I didn't have Take 7 yet, so I didn't know how to handle it. I channeled all my feelings into resentment and hate.

I didn't know how I could move forward. I felt so stuck. Remember we talked about releasing anger? I had to do a lot of anger release to move through that.

With some encouragement from my coach, I wrote a letter to my stepdad. It took some time. It was more for me than for him. But I did send it. I apologized for things I'd said about him. Then I thanked him for who he'd been in my life. He'd been an important force for those twenty years. While I didn't approve of his life choice and told him so, my bitterness was only hurting me. Forgiving him and thanking him set me free. Are we buddies now? No. But do I have ill will toward him? No, I truly don't. I pray for him and hope he has a long, happy life. Gratitude truly set me free.

Moving through tougher situations—such as the one with my stepdad—has made my gratitude muscle stronger. Practicing the power of gratitude was new to me back then. Now, because I use Take 7 so often, it has become ingrained. I create space for thanks quickly. I know now how good it feels on the other side. I truly, deeply believe everything happens *for* me, not *to* me. In everything that happens, there's a gift for me; I just have to find it. It's almost like a game—finding the thing to be grateful for in whatever happens.

Gratitude doesn't let those who hurt you off the hook. This isn't about them. It's about you. You can show compassion for Little You, for how you've survived, for what you've learned, for how your experiences have shaped who you are today. And you can start to make space for gratitude.

## How to Make Space for Gratitude

My walk-in closet is empty.

Okay, I'm exaggerating a little. It just seems empty because Cassie was here. She walked out with armloads of clothes, shoes, and purses. Cassie's business is turning handbags, shoes, and wore-it-once dresses into cash. She's a genius at it. She and I went through my closet and selected things I didn't need anymore that she could sell. So much of that stuff was not serving anymore. Now I've got all this room! To be honest, part of me wants to go shopping! Before I do, I'm going to take stock of what I already have and why I love it. Otherwise, I'd just fill it up randomly and find myself stuck again. For now I'm enjoying the space. I could have a dance party in here!

I'm hoping you feel like dancing too. You probably feel room in your chest. You've freed up so much space inside—mental and emotional space! And like me with my closet, you may feel the urge to go fill it up again. Let's use this opportunity to consciously choose what you allow into your newly available emotional space.

Making space for gratitude is an expression of strength and worth. What you have been through is shaping who you're going to be—if you let it! Looking at your timeline and reframing it shows you that you are uniquely equipped for your calling. You're stronger, you have resilience, you have deeper innovation and insight because of what you have been through.

Some people don't regret the past—instead, they get hung up on it. They romanticize it. They can't imagine a better future. This mindset tells them things were better before they grew up, or before that relationship ended, or before that loss, before whatever. I've been there. I can go there too. Call that for what it is: scarcity thinking. The best way to overcome that is with gratitude.

I'm thankful for the Little Me who believed, "I need more money." You're probably thinking that makes no sense, but stick with me. Having this mindset helped me at fourteen years old decide that I wanted to be a nurse because there was a nursing shortage. To Little Me, that meant there would always be a steady job for her. Becoming a nurse taught me so many things. It gave me authority to be a health expert at twenty-three years old. That authority helped me build a multimillion-dollar health coaching business via social media—in only three years. I wouldn't be where I am today if I had made different choices. So I am thankful for my time as a nurse, and I'm also thankful that I realized it wasn't the right path for me long term.

When you make space for thanks—for where you are now and where you have been—you come to a state of full acceptance. You accept all the parts of you that make you who you are. The gifts you've been given and the tough situations you've lived through set you up to be your champion self.

Little You in the "before" wasn't ready for what's next. Go to her and let her know you're grateful for the gifts of "before." You get to move through your life story, not around it. You get to move through the disappointment, the emotion, the trials. Gratitude springs from the awareness that you are who you are because of

When you make
space for thanks—
for where you are
now and where you
have been—you
come to a state of
full acceptance.

your experiences. Gratitude closes the distance between Little You and the person you are today.

## Practicing Gratitude

It's time to explore, dig in, and practice some gratitude. We're going to get loud with thanks! Grab something to write with—your journal or notes in your phone—and say *thanks*.

Thank God for it all. Thank him for your kids. Thank him for the people closest to you—by name. Get specific about why you are thankful for these people. You'll be surprised by what comes to mind when you get specific.

Here are some areas of your life where you might be able to say thanks.

- **Gifts of connections.** What organizations, businesses, conferences, or meetings led to meaningful connections?
- **Gifts of increased influence.** Where have you seen your reach expanded? Where has your territory grown? Recall critical moments where you made connections. Where did you last break through to new levels of influence?
- **Teaching relationships.** What mentors, coaches, or teachers have spoken into your life? What about good exits? Have there been negative forces in your life who've left?
- **Financial provisions.** Do you have someplace to live? Food to eat? Are your basic needs being met?
- **Skills—technical and relational.** What are you good at? Have you received training from someone in a craft or trade?

- **Music.** Are there songs that fortify you? Songs that lift you up? Songs that inspire you?
- **Podcasts.** Have you benefited from the wisdom or research of podcasts? Who are the people who put on those podcasts? What about their guests?
- **Experiences.** What's an adventure you've had that is meaningful to you? Have you been anyplace that changed your perspective or worldview?
- **Gifts of character.** What have you had to overcome? Have you persisted in something and gained grit or perseverance?
- **Gifts of wisdom.** Has experience made you wise, and if so, how?
- **Gifts of personal growth.** Take stock of the unique problems you've faced and challenges you've overcome on your journey. Again, it'll be helpful to consider your timeline. Lift up gratitude for the ways you've changed and grown as a person.

As certain people or things come to mind, pay attention. That may be the Holy Spirit prompting you to act. To reach out.

Give that gratitude away with open hands. Send a thank-you note. Send a text. Call. Send flowers. Send a gift card. What matters is that you find a way to bless others with your gratitude. As an example, I met a woman a decade ago who touched my life at a conference. I thought of her today and didn't even know if I had her number anymore, but I looked her up in my phone, and there it was. I called her to thank her right then. Our conversation was short, not more than five minutes. Honestly it was the best five minutes of my day. That interaction gave me such a good feeling inside. She would never have known if I didn't act on that impulse—but I'd have missed out on such a sweet moment.

Give what you want to get. Whatever you wish to receive, give it away. This is a principle I find to be true in so many areas. By turning attention to giving whatever it is you wish to give, you make space for those things to come into your life. Maybe you want to be financially fruitful. If so, ask, *How can I help somebody else get rich today?* Maybe you do that by buying something from your favorite podcaster or buying an author's book. Maybe you want to be successful in your business. Then ask, *How am I supporting other small businesses?* If I want to have better friends, the question is, *How am I being a better friend? How am I showing up for the friends in my life?* If you want to have a better marriage or to have a better spouse, ask, *How am I being a better spouse?*

It's not about giving to get. It's about gratefully participating in a life of abundance.

In the next chapter the sixth question of Take 7 will build on the previous five: the practice of **listening** to your feelings, **getting curious** about what drives you, **nurturing** yourself, **reframing** your perspective, and **giving thanks** for all that's happened *for* you (not *to* you). Making space for the gratitude creates a way forward. We see how we've been guided and gifted. An attitude of gratitude makes space to answer question 6: "What do I *really* want?"

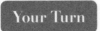

## Radical Gratitude

- Decide to reach out to one person today to tell them what you're grateful for and why. You can do this with a text, a call, a letter, a package, or even a visit. The beautiful thing about extending gratitude this way is that it blesses the giver as much as the recipient!
- What are you grateful for? Name at least one thing each that you can see, smell, touch, taste, and hear.
- Phone check: Take a look at the last few things you took a photo of. Why are you grateful for these things?

*Chapter Ten*

# Deep Desire

## *Question 6: What Do I Really Want?*

Now is the time to know that God is able. To connect
your current reality with God's present ability.

—PRISCILLA SHIRER

ONE OF MY PROUDEST ACHIEVEMENTS IN LIFE IS
that I participated in the miracle of creating three actual human
beings. I was hyperaware of what my body needed when I was
pregnant with each of my kids. I *craved* certain foods. I didn't
have to think about it—my body told me what it needed. Bananas.
Peanut butter. Everything bagels. The necessary ingredients to
fuel this baby making occurred to me effortlessly. I listened to my
own needs and satisfied them without guilt.

Only *you* know what's good for you. That's something I come back to again and again: trust in yourself. Question 6 is about tuning in to your heart's desire and asking, *What do I really want?*

Notice this isn't about what you *should* want. Resist the urge to "should" yourself. This is about paying attention to what you desire at a bone-deep level. By listening to your desires, you can craft a life of abundance that's uniquely you. Only you can say what that will look like. You're going to have to get quiet—tune out other voices—to answer this question. Look inside for the answer. Don't go to the people around you, looking to them to tell you what you want, what you desire. Looking outside for fulfillment and happiness is a distraction. You can't find your heart's desire by checking out your phone to see what other people are doing to make themselves happy. Or seeking outside direction or approval. You can't live out someone else's purpose. Looking around won't show you the desire of your heart.

## The Sky's the Limit

Imagine you could snap your fingers and instantly be where you want with whomever you want doing whatever you want. What would that look like for you? Answering honestly will illuminate what's important to you. It's a way to use your imagination for good to see what things light you up. Or we can put it another way: If you could wake up tomorrow happy and excited for what the day holds, what would that day look like?

You must check in with yourself. Look inside to discover the life of your dreams. Your deepest desire will point you in the right direction. When you're living life with purpose and love, riches of abundance, meaning, and connection will always follow.

Your heart's desires aren't random. They're placed in there by God. Gratitude for how you're wired gives you clarity on the desires of your heart. Your deep desire will always be in alignment with how God has made you and how your journey has shaped you.

These two questions will provide clarity on your heart's desire.

- **What lights you up?** As you expressed gratitude, themes may have emerged for you. As you looked at your timeline, certain events or activities spoke to you. Look for those sparks of joy.
- **Who brings out your champion self?** What you're doing matters a lot, but it also matters a lot who you're with. Who do you want to be around? Who will you be serving or coming alongside? The sky's the limit here. You may not have access to the people in the rooms you want to be in right now, but if you dream it, you can achieve it. The *who* matters.

Knowing *what* lights you up and *who* brings out your best self is going to make a big difference as you go forward. You can begin to avoid the things that don't light you up and avoid partnering with or spending too much time with those who don't bring out your best self. Most of all, the clarity you gain from being honest with yourself about these questions will illuminate your path forward because you can start to consciously curate your life. By answering from your gut, you'll be moving in the direction of a life more fully in tune with the person you were made to be.

It's important in this step to find out what Little You wants *and* what your champion self wants. For me, when it comes to the "I need more money" story, Little Me deeply wanted to just be a kid. You know how they say ignorance is bliss? Little kids shouldn't have to worry about adult issues. Little Me at eight years old just wanted to play volleyball outside with her friends. So what do I do when I'm stuck, to nurture my inner child? I pull out a volleyball and head to the courts in my neighborhood to let her be a kid. Then champion Cayla can decide what she really wants right now.

## Growth from Cravings

Your life will inevitably change as you listen to and pursue the desire of your heart. Your desire may lead you to minor, incremental changes nobody notices but you. Or you might decide to make a radical change to the existing structure of your life to better align with who you're meant to be. You are the decider here. You decide how your life is going to look as you pursue your heart's desire.

There's also the possibility that your craving may be satisfied when you explore a new side hustle or embark on a new hobby or develop a talent or skill.

For example, my client Felicity earned a master of business in finance from a prestigious university, then she went on to serve as CFO for a medical services company. As she went through Take 7, she realized her craving to grow something tangible and real. She decided to plant a garden. As a child, she and her family planted a vegetable garden together each summer.

Little Felicity thought of gardening as tedious and boring when her parents made her work in the yard. It had seemed like a pointless chore. But something about seeing the literal fruits of her labor stuck with her. All these years later, as she worked with numbers and in relationships for a living, she recognized a desire to produce something beautiful. She wanted a garden. So Felicity sketched out plans all week. Then on Saturday she woke up early, drove to a big box store to pick out plants, and loaded her SUV up with fertilizer, flats of vegetables and annuals, and a dozen large terra-cotta pots. Felicity planted the flowers and vegetables in the twelve containers on her back porch where they could get plenty of sun.

Her life is fuller now. She still runs the finances of the firm, earning a great living, but gardening provides abundance of a different sort in her life. She's joined a club that tends a community garden where they swap seeds, stories, and produce. The other gardening club members are very different from her. They aren't people she'd normally meet in her professional or social circles, so she's pushed outside her comfort zone sometimes, but in ways she reports as healthy and joy filled. She's growing all the time.

When you have clarity about what you desire, you have focus. You don't get distracted. And you have power because you're where you're designed to be. Felicity's friends at work may think she's bananas for hanging out on the weekends with the gardening club. But what might seem like foolishness to them doesn't matter. She's living in her purpose. She's using her unique set of gifts and talents. She's courageous and strong.

When you have

clarity about

what you desire,

you have focus.

It can be uncomfortable for those around you when you grow (and Felicity is growing, literally and figuratively!). But you don't need permission from others. You don't need their approval. All you need is to admit *to yourself* that you're ready to grow. Ready for something new. That realization can be life-giving. Your desires will shift in your heart as you grow. Pay attention. That may be the Holy Spirit.

Where do you desire growth? (Remember, there is no wrong answer here. Trust yourself.) Let's look again at the Freedom Wheel you used for a life audit in chapter 3.

- Health
- Wealth
- Career
- Spiritual Life
- Romantic Life
- Family Life
- Social Life

What you deeply desire may not be listed here. Feel free to make up your own list! Allow yourself to imagine a life where you wake up energized and excited. You're purposeful. Connected. And physically strong. Curious about what the day holds. What would that look like?

I continue to do regular check-ins with myself using Take 7. One summer I had a huge breakthrough. I was born and raised in the town where we were living at the time. I'd built my health and wellness business there, had my three babies there, and I had a Monday morning cooking show on the local news. It was home. But something was off. I went through Take 7. *What's not working for me?*

The summers in Bakersfield were long and hot. One of my best friends lived a block away and yet was now completely out of my life. When I drove the streets of downtown, I got all kinds of triggered around traumatic things in my childhood. I'm the queen of positivity, but where I lived kept reminding me of my past. It didn't represent where I was headed in my future.

The Little Me that was showing up felt like a victim. She was never going to feel safe and sit in the back seat in an environment that didn't represent a bright future for her.

Now, I had no idea where I was going to make it happen or how our family of five would handle it, but I had a vision of moving. My husband, Chase, and I had a serious dream. We took a family trip to Portland, Oregon, to visit another family that had moved there. They seemed so happy, and it was exciting to experience a new city with our kids. We knew Portland was not our destination, but we had clarity: we were going to move. So we tried a couple cities as a family on vacation. We decided on Newport Beach, California. Within two weeks our house was up for sale, and we signed a lease on a house with ocean views from every room.

Your dreams move quick when you start showing up as your champion self while loving on Little You at the same time. My inner child needed a new environment as much as my champion self required it.

## Less Is More

Maybe what you desire doesn't look like "more." That's great! "I want less" is a legitimate desire too. Emily Ley talked about this when she was on my podcast. She'd spent years building her company and realizing her vision, and she'd reached a point where she had a craving for a break. She decided to take a sabbatical where she pulled away for several months from the business, social media, and traveling.

What exactly would *less* look like for you? Allow yourself permission to explore that possibility. One client had an amazing career in business and a flourishing personal life. She had earned a reputation as a leader in her field. When her boss offered her a major promotion, she took the opportunity to say, "Thanks for your belief in me. I have a vision for a new job in the company where I do some of what I do now but offload the rest onto someone else." Instead of looking for more prestige and money, she made a lateral move where she had more flexibility. Not only is she happier, but the company also got to keep a valued employee.

## Overcoming Resistance to Change

You're getting creative, casting a vision, and that's a beautiful thing. As you do this, you may find that you resist change. If you feel resistance around going for your dream, ask yourself, *Should a tree feel guilty reaching for the sun or down into the soil for nutrients?* No. Trees naturally live out their purpose. When they thrive, we all thrive. That's the way we're made.

It breaks my heart to see women shrink back or try to make

themselves small. Imagine if a tree did that! How absurd. Making yourself small and shrinking doesn't glorify God or bring God pleasure. He longs to give you, his daughter, the desire of your heart.

Maybe Little You resists change because she worries about loss. Turn your attention to the Little You who's showing up when you worry or get nervous around change. Which Little You is showing up? How old is she? What's she going through?

Imagine just packing up everything and moving across the country without telling your family what's happening. They'd freak out, right? That's how it is with Little You. She needs your assurance. She needs to know you're paying attention and you hear her concerns. Nurture her. Push through resistance by providing her proof that change will be positive—that life will be better.

Close your eyes and envision sitting down in a place where your inner child feels comfortable. Imagine her sitting with you. Share your vision. Show her evidence of other people accomplishing something cool like this and that it's safe. Explain what life will look like when your vision is a reality. Paint a picture for her. Get crystal clear on what that is. Assure her that *life will get better. This is safe. It's good. There's nothing to fear.*

No more playing it small. It's time to choose faith over fear. Envision your dream until it's reality.

## What's Your Dream?

What do *you* desire? We can have all different type of dreams. What's that dream that's on your heart right now? It can be anything. In any category. Write it. Envision it!

Write what your dream will look like when it comes to fruition. Get as specific as you can. There's a neuro-linguistic programming (NLP) technique I want to teach you that we call scripting. The idea is that if you write out exactly how you want your life to play out, it's more likely to happen. According to NLP, descriptive words activate parts of our subconscious. By using your imagination this way, you're showing your mind that there are possibilities outside of your current situation and what you're going through. I'll ask some leading questions to get you started. Let's get your imagination and creativity flowing. Soon you'll see your desired reality come into focus—and then you can step into it.

1. Imagine how your body feels when your desired outcome is met. What is your energy like?
2. Are you relaxed or excited?
3. What are you wearing?
4. Are you moving quickly, slowly, or are you still?
5. What are the sounds?
6. What's the lighting like? What textures and smells are you experiencing?

Here's an example from Marie.

I empower women to feel and look their best by providing high-end salon experiences. We use organic products in a serene, light-drenched, plant-rich environment. I wear all-black, loose-fitting clothes and my feet are bare on the cool marble floors. The pace is relaxed and easy, filled with positive energy. Soothing music plays from hidden speakers tucked into the woodwork. I work alongside other aestheticians who are collaborative and creative. Our exclusive clients subscribe to our services, which allows us to have scheduled, unhurried visits.

Visualize your dream often—daily, if possible. And keep a visual reminder of your "scripted" desire.

I envision my desired reality every morning. I collaborate with the ultimate Creator, asking for blessing and favor on the vision. God often surprises me, pointing out people and opportunities that will help make my vision a reality.

I'm a visual learner, so something that's been super helpful for me is my vision board app that I look at every day. It's electronic instead of the old-fashioned way. It has reminders—like I am a *New York Times* bestselling author. Those reminders make me smile and keep me motivated to realize my dream.

Marie used her journal to envision her dream. She sketched out her ideas for her salon. She cut out pictures from magazines and catalogs. Today she's achieved a beautiful, multilocation spa. She even created her own skincare product line. I love that she went above and beyond what she first thought was possible. Flipping through the pages of her journal reminds her of how her vision is evolving and growing—and how she's realizing that vision daily.

## Protection

You have a unique desire and purpose. Your desire gave birth to a vision. Hold it close. Nourish it like you would a newborn baby.

God often surprises
me, pointing
out people and
opportunities that
will help make my
vision a reality.

Be careful not to share your vision too early. It's a precious and vulnerable gift, not to be taken lightly.

When you're ready to share your vision, choose who you share it with carefully. I've shared a vision too soon and regretted it. People can be brutal. A few years ago, I had an idea that I was excited about. I naively talked about it too soon. I shared with someone on my network marketing team who said she wanted to help me, but, in reality, she took that idea and monetized it under her brand. I'd shared my vision too early and with the wrong person. Now I know.

It's time to feed your vision. Start by giving your vision shape. I recommend a vision board for this. There are a ton available online. Canva has several. I like the *Why* vision board app for my phone, but there are at least a dozen others available in the app store. Use the one you like best.

If you're not into screens, you can represent your vision another way. If you've got a product idea, come up with a prototype. Liz's vision for a line of healthy snacks took shape when she printed out labels with a logo designed on her laptop. She printed them, then pasted them onto bottles and packages to give herself a sense of what her vision would look like. She's working daily to make that vision a reality, and when she sees those protypes on her kitchen counter, it reminds her conscious mind that she's making her dream come to life.

Your dreams are precious to you and they're precious to God. Offer up your vision to God daily and invite his favor and blessing. Protect your vision by praying over it daily. Your vision is threatening to the Enemy because you're aligning yourself with kingdom work. Pray specifically for protection.[1] You and only you know what will satisfy your God-given desire. Only you can birth that vision.

Once you have a dream, know that it's bound to change over time. Dreams grow as we do and as the world changes. Lean into that and be excited by it. Keep revisiting your vision and then start taking steps to make it a reality.

When you have a healthy relationship with yourself, what matters most to you comes into focus. You notice your feelings and can **voice** a complaint. You **get curious** about why you've accepted less than you deserve. You **nurture** your inner child. You have perspective that comes from **reframing**. Your perspective creates space for **thanks**. Your **desire** gives birth to a vison or goal. The final Take 7 question invites you to **act** in a way that moves you closer to your goal. Question 7 is, "What is the best next step for me?"

## Baking with Sourdough

Forrest Gump said life is like a box of chocolates, but for me, life is like a good sourdough. Stay with me here. This is going to make sense, I promise!

My mother-in-law gave me some sourdough starter that had been given to her. Seriously? This starter is gold. It's the real deal, passed down through a bunch of friends, and it makes the best bread.

## Sourdough Bread Recipe

I love a good sourdough. But the starter is fussy! I feed it flour and water every day. When it's active and bubbly—like it's about to bust out of the jar—it's ready to be used for this recipe.

### INGREDIENTS

2 3/4 cups warm water

3 3/4 teaspoons salt

7 1/2 cups all-purpose flour

1 1/2 cups mature sourdough starter

### DIRECTIONS

1. Mix together the warm water, salt, and flour. Mix gently—it's so finicky—and let the dough rest for 30 minutes.

2. Add the sourdough starter. Don't dump it in—just dimple it, setting some aside to use later. Poke the starter into the dough.

3. Mix the dough by hand for about 3 minutes, being careful not to overmix. Cover it with plastic wrap and let it sit for 30 minutes.

4.  Stretch and fold the dough and let it sit again. Do this six times—every 30 minutes.
5.  Put your dough in the fridge. I let mine sit in there for three days.
6.  Take the cold dough out of the fridge, put it onto a lightly floured board, and shape it into a ball. Be careful not to pop any bubbles. Refrigerate it again overnight. Then let it come back to room temperature.
7.  Finally, pop the dough into a hot Dutch oven. Bake at 500 degrees for 28 minutes, and voila! It's the best bread you ever tasted in your life.

Making good sourdough bread takes intention. It takes care. It can even be a bit tedious. The thing is, once you experience it, it's so good. All that intention and care are worth every second. That's how it is with your life. If you want your vision for your life to thrive, protect it, feed it, and maintain it. And like my sourdough, it's so worth it!

## Chapter Eleven

# Act Now

*Question 7: What Is the Best Next Step for Me?*

Advance confidently in the direction of your dreams.

—HENRY DAVID THOREAU

GOING AFTER WHAT YOU REALLY WANT LOOKS inspired. It's purposeful. It's literally love in action.

It takes courage to act in the direction of your dreams. Don't be intimidated by that. You're made for it! You're leading yourself with love with your champion self in the driver's seat.

Acting in the direction of your dreams isn't about perfection. Perfect is an illusion. I want to encourage you to take messy action. Let it be messy—that's okay! Just take steps in the right direction. One step at a time will get you to your destination.

## Messy Action

Michelle is a great example. She worked in the medical field as a nurse practitioner. She'd trained rigorously for the job and was successful at it. But she felt stuck. The limitations of the industry were frustrating to her. She hated not being able to connect with her clients because of the way conventional medical practices are set up. By working through Take 7, Michelle identified what she really wanted. She wanted to have meaningful interactions with her clients, helping them to better health on her own terms. Her desire shaped her vision for a concierge women's medical practice.

Michelle continued working as a nurse for six months, putting money aside, while she wrote up a business plan. She set up an LLC, copyrighted a logo, and procured all the necessary supplies she'd need to launch her new venture. Did she get everything perfect? She would tell you absolutely not! She made lots of mistakes along the way, but she was determined to let failure be her teacher. Today she's realized her vision. She runs a seven-figure business. She's passionate about innovative healthcare and wakes up every day excited to learn, grow, and serve. She connects with other women, impacting lives, generating wealth, and creating a legacy for the future.

Michelle's story reminds us that a life isn't transformed overnight, but with intention, it can radically change. You can move in the direction of your dream today. Action breeds clarity. Schedule it. Make "me time" part of your daily routine when you work toward your vision.

Here are some tips to get you started on taking action.

1. **Commit to Being a Learner.** You can learn literally anything. Learn how to start a business by reading a book or watching videos on YouTube. When you learn, you expand your horizons. And put what you're learning into action. Even before your situation changes, *you* have changed by the knowledge you've gained. And isn't that what it's all about?

2. **Find Your People.** The right people make a huge difference. With the right people to affirm you, remind you of your worth, and provide emotional support, you can achieve anything. Your people may already be gathered; if not, seize the opportunity to be the one to gather them. Remember: authenticity attracts. Fake and phony repels your tribe.

3. **Act as If.** Act as if you have stepped into your destiny. Be that person now. Your dreams will become your reality if you decide to be the person you're destined to be today. You don't have to wait till you have all the things or the perfect circumstances to live out your best life. If you wait for the perfect anything, you'll be waiting for the rest of your life—and maybe even die with the regrets of having never acted on your desires. Decide on the characteristics of your ideal life, then get living that way now. I'm currently taking piano lessons. Instead of saying, "I'm trying to become a piano player," I say, "I play the piano." I'm still learning, so saying it this way helps me remember that this is becoming part of my identity. I even visualize myself playing in Carnegie Hall as I say it.

4. **Dress the Part.** When you're going after what you really

You don't have

to wait till you

have all the things

or the perfect

circumstances to live

out your best life.

want, demonstrate your confidence and self-respect by showing up looking like a million bucks. If I'm looking to sign lucrative deals, do you think that'll happen if I'm wearing sweats and have my hair in a ball cap? No! It's important that I walk in with confidence and self-assurance. What colors do you feel most empowered in? Don't wear what makes you feel comfortable. Wear what makes you say *yes* to you. Make sure you look like you could walk in and slay, then walk in and stay!

5. **Be Prepared to Sacrifice.** Achieving your vision may require giving up what's good in exchange for what's great. I sold my home to finance my first company. Selling our dream home was hard, but I knew that to get ahead we'd need to step back for a bit. Remind yourself that starting something is admirable. To go up, you'll need to give something up. It might be unhealthy relationships, it might be limiting beliefs, it might be time, it might be money. For me, the sacrifice has been worth it, 100 percent! It didn't happen overnight. Let's normalize the notion that you're not going to instantly see your dream come true. You'll need to put in some sweat equity for it. But when you know you're going for what you *really* want, it's worth it.

6. **Keep Persisting.** Persistence is everything. Just showing up makes the difference—whether it's in health, wealth, spirituality, career, or relationships. Consistency yields results.

Taking action looks different for each of us, but it's always about taking intentional steps in the direction of your specific vision. With intention, you'll get there!

## Taking Action

In this chapter we'll walk through the Freedom Wheel and decide what action you need to take in each category in order to live abundantly. I'll also give you some tools in each area that you can use as you answer question seven. By taking a holistic approach, you can act to grow in one area that will also feed the others!

# 1. HEALTH

A client that I had worked with for a while, Jasmine, was successful in so many areas but she knew she wasn't living her healthiest life. When she found out her sister was pregnant, she was motivated to make a change. She imagined taking her future niece or nephew to the park, blowing bubbles outside, jumping on a trampoline, and riding bikes. That's what abundant health looked like for Jasmine. That vision motivated her to act. She hired a trainer. She started making healthy choices, acting as if she was already living in abundant health. She trained her body's strength and endurance for that future relationship with her niece or nephew. Jasmine wasn't going to accidentally live her best life. She chose to act in ways that usher in abundant health—and it worked.

Imagine yourself living in abundant health. What comes to mind? What characteristics of a healthy lifestyle matter to you? There are no wrong answers here! It's about what *you* want to feel in your body. How will you feel when you wake up? Do you want to be filled with energy? What foods will you consume that give you that energy? What foods that make you feel tired can you avoid?

When I do a health audit, I like to use quantitative measures to check growth. I have recently been working on getting all my hormones optimized because all of a sudden I was sweating through my sheets at night and getting less than three hours of sleep. I tried no caffeine and no blue light before bed, and a little melatonin gummy before sleep, but nothing was helping. Fortunately, my functional medicine doctor discovered that my progesterone was extremely low. So I started taking a low dose of progesterone and within two nights I started sleeping better! I'm excited to see how the quality of my sleep improves along with all of my other labs when I go in for checkups. Now I have a baseline, which I think is important if you are wanting to track your growth—not just in health but in all the areas of Take 7.

## 2. WEALTH

What about abundant wealth? Maybe, like me, you *love* what you do daily that provides a good living for yourself and your people. I believe I could do this every day for the rest of my life, *but* I want options. If you don't find a way to make money in your sleep, you will work until you die. Having the option to choose is important to me.

Are you taking steps toward your vision of abundant wealth? Have you given yourself permission to envision what that will even look like? When I encourage my clients to dream, I say, "What would it look like if you did *not* work every day? What if you were living your dream life? What would you need to make that dream a reality?"

What's the gap between your income and your lifestyle expenses? Draft a personal financial vision. Decide what you can do now to act in the direction of that vision.

## 3. CAREER

What about your career? If you had unlimited potential in your career, what would you do? What would you create?

My friend owns a trash company. It's an extremely lucrative business. Does she love trash? Not even close. But does she love managing a team, offering steady jobs for that team, and providing a good living for their families? One hundred percent. She's proud to have obtained city contracts that allow amazing employees job security, and because of that, the city's residents have reliable trash pickups. It's a win-win. She's become obsessed with acquiring all the skills she needs to run a successful business: culture, teamwork, sales, and operations. She invested in her greatest asset, and that's made so many lives better!

Discover the meaning for *you* in your career, then become obsessed with being the best at that skill or process. Decide on one step you can take today toward a life where you feel what you do matters.

## 4. SPIRITUAL LIFE

What about spiritual abundance? Rate your spiritual life on a scale of 1–10 with 1 being "constant state of fear and doubt" and 10 being "living in a state of abundant faith and praise." There is no right or wrong answer here. This is about self-awareness.

Consider what you can do to take a step in the direction you want your life to go. Give yourself permission to act with intention in your spiritual life.

Tricia rated herself a 2 when she considered her spiritual life. That wasn't in line with her vision of spiritual abundance. She decided to nurture the kernel of faith she'd neglected for years,

176

so she carved out ten minutes a day to read and pray. It wasn't a lot, but she stuck with it. Recently she went on her first silent retreat—three days devoted to prayer and reflection. Major breakthroughs happened on this retreat, releasing Tricia from strongholds of anxiety and worry. That happened because Tricia took daily, small steps in the direction of her vision. What step can you take today to move in the direction of your vision for spiritual abundance?

## 5. ROMANTIC LIFE

Using Take 7 to self-coach through hiccups in your marriage can be extremely effective. The dynamic shifts when you do that self-work instead of simply noticing your feelings and then refusing to do anything about them. Strong, healthy relationships don't happen accidentally. Get intentional about what you value in a partner and in a relationship. Decide what abundance in your romantic life will look like for you. You don't have to follow someone else's rulebook. Realize a vision for your relationship that's custom made!

## 6. FAMILY LIFE

The world will try to tell you what families should look like, but your vision for what abundance looks like in your family is unique to you. You'll need to get honest with yourself, using Take 7, to determine what you *really* want. For you, acting in the direction of that vision may look like creating some healthy boundaries. It may look like carving out scheduled time with specific people. It may even involve mending relationships. Only you can answer that. Take 7 to figure it out and then *act*.

You don't
have to follow
someone else's
rulebook. Realize
a vision for your
relationship that's
custom made!

## 7. SOCIAL LIFE

My first-ever business coach asked me to rate myself in the friendship department. I was surprised. We were supposed to be growing my career, weren't we? It was a good challenge. It showed me that I'd been so focused on other areas of my life that I'd completely neglected personal friendships. My friendship love tank was empty. I realized I had been telling myself a scarcity story. I'd been limited by the belief that there were no good people available. Logically that could not be true.

I always say to give what you want to receive. So I wrote down the characteristics I value in a friend. Then I asked myself the hard question: "Do I have these characteristics?" One characteristic I'd written down was loyalty. If I want loyalty, I need to be loyal. For me that looks like being loyal to my values. I chose to honor my values, and I look for friends who share and respect similar values.

## Take 7 Life Audits

Not long ago I was using Take 7 to do a life audit. As I was reviewing the Freedom Wheel, something began to stir inside me. I'd started Mommy Millionaire to help more women become millionaires. I'd grown my team and my dream became reality. Together we achieved goals I never could have dreamed of just a decade ago. I'm so proud of us!

As I was writing this book, I felt something inside that said, "You're made for more." I resisted it at first. It seemed ridiculous to think that the abundance I was experiencing wasn't enough. But it occurred to me that I needed to practice what I preach.

179

I coached myself through Take 7 in a deliberate way, doing the deeper dive. I checked in with Little Me and realized she'd begun placing so much stock in the word "millionaire." My identity had gotten entangled with that word. It bothered me that I'd tied myself to "millionaire." There is nothing implicitly wrong with that word. I'm not ashamed of financial worth—far from it.

But what had once been a dream had become a limitation. As I explored the space for gratitude in my life, I returned again and again to my passion for real estate and investing. That part of my life brings me so much joy, abundance, connection, and purpose.

Then one night I was walking around my neighborhood, praying like I usually do. I was pleading with God. *Show me your will for my life, Lord. Everything feels heavy. Show me your ways, Lord.* I felt this instant voice saying, *It's time to move on.*

*Move on from what, Lord?* My spirit knew, but I was scared to say it. I finally asked, *Mommy Millionaire?*

Radio silence.

I kept walking. I kept praying. *Jesus, Jesus, Jesus.*

*Everybody is so focused on making money, they've forgotten to make a life.* I had this epiphany that I was no longer aligned with my own company. I was no longer living in abundance because I was out of alignment.

I believe it's important to create so many assets that you truly can experience time freedom. Real estate investing is what lights me up. Even after I became financially abundant in my late twenties, the way I stayed free was by investing the income I was making into real estate. Assets that are insured, protected, and secured.

As I shared what I was discovering with a girlfriend in my

Bible study group, she encouraged me to consider a rebrand. The idea struck me as both obvious and brilliant. I prayed about it and felt a conviction: it was the right move. Now the question was how to execute.

When I told my team my desire, they were extremely supportive. We began brainstorming ideas. In what some might describe as a coincidence—but I believe it was a divine confirmation—my friend Natalia at Join the Social Studio reached out to say, "Hey, I want to rebrand you for free to thank you for blessing my life." Incredible. How do you even explain that confirmation? Thank you, God!

This new iteration of my company is a natural extension of my desire to help women achieve financial freedom and generational wealth. It's a fruit of that work in my life. When we announced the rebrand, I cried a little—but only a little! Little Me had worked so hard to build that original brand. Letting go of what doesn't fit anymore is worth doing—and worth celebrating. Little Me didn't want to let go at first. Now she's proud and happy. I'm grateful for where we've been, and I couldn't be happier about where we're headed.

Schedule time in your calendar to make a routine of taking that next step. Take messy action!

Your Turn

## Time to Act

When you voiced your complaint, it involved one of the areas on the Freedom Wheel. Your vision answers the deep desire inside you—a desire unique to you. Move toward your vision today. You won't get there overnight, but intention and consistency will get you there.

The following are ideas for actions to move you in the direction of the life of your dreams.

## Health

Earlier we talked about protecting and investing in your biggest asset. What will it look like for you to protect and invest in your health?

In my experience, when it comes to vibrant health, people underrate sleep (and overrate food). Here's a checklist for healthy sleep:

- **No electronics before bed.** Stopping all screen use two hours before bed is best. Try reading fiction to engage the imagination. It helps turn off the thoughts and concerns of the day.
- **Make your bedroom a sanctuary.** Don't do anything else in that room.
- **Keep it cool.** The ideal sleeping temperature is around 68 degrees.
- **Outfit your bed with comfy linens.** I like cotton sheets and silk pillowcases.
- **Brain dump.** If you have trouble shutting down your thoughts at night—like so many of us—do a brain dump of everything that

needs to be done the following day. Once it's all out on paper, triage your list. Decide what's most important and what can wait. Creating focus and intention for the next day will allow you to sleep like a baby so you can wake up and slay the day!

# Wealth

I have three key practices for managing finances.

- **Clarity.** If you're working on increasing your wealth, the number-one most important thing you can do is to figure out where you're currently at financially. Clarity is key.
- **Alignment.** Next, create alignment. What matters to you? It's up to you to allocate where your money goes. Align your priorities with your spending. Don't just pay your bills and then impulsively decide what to do with the remaining money. Be intentional. Create an alignment plan (aka budget) and begin to align your spending with your priorities.[i]
- **Invest.** I don't know your financial situation, but I can tell you that the average American is $96,000 in debt.[1] The fastest way to experience financial freedom is to build up your investing muscle. Yes, even when you're in debt! So many people think eliminating debt is the biggest thing, but that alone won't build wealth. I'm not against debt; I'm against being enslaved to debt.

   To be financially free, you have to invest. Decide what's right for you, then begin to invest in an asset, even if it's a tiny bit at first.

---

i. Go to caylacraft.com for a free download that helps you calculate your net worth *and* create an alignment plan.

Train that investing muscle. Even 1 percent of your income matters. You can gradually work toward investing 25 percent of your income. That's the way to really build your wealth.

Here are some other practical tips for increasing wealth:

- Don't use a debit card. Cut it up. Pay cash for things that are in your alignment plan.
- If you own a business, use a business credit card for all business expenses. (There are benefits, plus protections if someone screws you over.)
- Cancel recurring subscriptions that aren't vital for your future.
- Try to max out your retirement plan annually.
- Self-direct your IRA or 401K.[ii]
- Get educated about what you want to invest in. The more educated you are, the more empowered you'll feel to make that investment.

## Career

Three actions can dramatically impact your career path.

- **Learn.** Ask yourself, How can I be the highest paid in my field? If you want to advance to that level, you must invest in the skill set you offer. Find out what training, education, or certification is required and pursue it.
- **Connect.** To grow in your career, you need to connect with people further along than you and let them know you're capable.

---

ii. For more on this, visit directedira.com/craft.

When I was a nurse, I took on extra training to advance my career. Taking classes and getting certifications allowed me the chance to be in the room with people who had decades more experience than me. When I got on the dean's radar, I asked to meet with her to learn more about advancing my career. That meeting led to a job that helped me advance even further.

- **Help others.** When it comes to networking, be what John David Mann calls a Go-giver. Walk into every situation with the mindset of helping others achieve their goals. Ask "What do you have going on?" and "What will make this year a win for you?"

## Spiritual Life

Have you ever seen the sign that says "Know God, Know Peace. No God, No Peace"?

It's true: the more you know God, the more you'll experience peace. The only way to really *know God* is to spend time with him. Invest in that relationship. The more you know God, the more you will hunger for time with him.

Here are some tips for how to grow in your spiritual life:

- **Talk to God first.** Go to God in prayer and in his Word before you go to anyone else with your issues. So often when we have a problem, we go to a friend. Learning to take it to God first is a game changer!
- **Spiritual community.** Committing to a group of other believers who are actively seeking God's will in his Word can make a huge impact. For me, this has been crucial. It helps me stay accountable in my spiritual life.

- **Pray together.** My husband and I pray together. It's part of our daily routine. It helps me feel peaceful even when things are going crazy around me. When we're rooted in God, nothing can shake us.
- **Find a pastor** who you trust and can be mentored by.
- **Play worship music.** It's amazing what a difference music can make!

## Romantic Life

Invest in your relationship with your spouse.

- **Focus on what matters most.** Decide what values are important to you in a spouse. Once you know what those attributes are, you will understand how to enhance your relationship in multiple ways. Express gratitude for your spouse in your mind, in prayer, and especially out loud or in writing to him. This is true for married couples and for single women with the desire to find that special someone. Focusing on the values and attributes that matter to you brings subconscious thoughts into the conscious mind, which helps that vision become a reality.

  Look for ways to support the traits you value most in him. For instance, it means so much to me that my husband is actively involved in our children's lives. He's an amazing dad. Expressing gratitude for that shared value helps me put everything else into perspective.
- **Prioritize your relationship.** We schedule the rest of our lives, so why would we assume our relationship with our spouse will happen accidentally? Intention matters. In my marriage, we've learned to schedule time for what matters most,

including intimacy, finances, problem-solving, and dreaming together. If we need to have a serious conversation, we eliminate distractions—and we discuss only one problem at a time. That focus is so important.

- **Invest in intimacy.** Healthy romantic relationships also require intimacy. I highly recommend that you identify what's not working with you in your intimacy by working through Take 7. So many of us have shame around sexual intimacy, and let me tell you, that's not from God. Sex is good. I coach my clients who want to make progress in this area to make time for growing in intimacy: schedule and prioritize it. Intention makes all the difference.

## Family Life

Carve out intentional time with family members.

- **Create family agreements** that everyone in the family commits to. For instance, we used to live next to my in-laws. When we first moved in, we came up with agreements that outlined our commitments. We asked that they call before they came to visit. They couldn't just show up. They didn't want that, though. They wanted us to show up at their house and just walk in whenever we wanted. That was an agreement we both upheld.

   Family agreements can also cover *how* to communicate when there is a disagreement. My father-in-law has always prided himself on the fact that his family is no drama. When I came in the picture, let's just say I brought the drama. If there was an elephant in the room, we were going to talk about it. It was like oil and water—the two don't mix. We had to come to an agreement on how we would discuss any problems we had with each other. We scheduled time to talk about it, so everyone knew and was prepared to come to a solution.

- **Family worship.** In addition to worship outside our home, we have worship time at home. My kids pray and Chase leads us in a worship song, then we read the Bible together and discuss it.

- **Honor regularly scheduled time together.** Some families eat dinner at the dinner table. I wish we could, but it's not realistic except for two nights a week for us. We set aside time in our cars to discuss our day and feelings. The point is to be intentional about talking with your kids and helping them feel comfortable communicating with you.

- **Schedule vacation time with family members you love.** We are in a transition in our family where our extended family lives in different cities. So we planned how we will get together in the next twelve months. Some will meet us at hockey tournaments when we are on their side of the country and we will do one vacation in a new destination together! Instead of being sad about being apart, we are excited to create new memories together.

## Social Life

Do you want to improve your friendships? Here are some tips.

- **Find a hobby you enjoy and join a club or league.** For example, my mom just moved to Newport Beach with me where, at sixty years old, she needs to make new friends. She loves pickleball, so she found a pickleball league to join and has met some really awesome people so far. You can create a book club with people in your neighborhood or kids' school friends' parents. Who knows, you might even go talk about the book!

- **Be intentional about friendships that you want to deepen.** Create scheduled time on your calendars for and with those people. I love to work out and I love my friends. So I schedule a few workouts or walks every week with my close friends. We can have our cake and eat it too, getting those health and social benefits at the same time!

- **Always look for reasons to celebrate people in your social circle.** Make deposits into the lives of people you truly care about. If someone gets a raise, throw a party at your house. Does a friend love lemons, and you see a dishtowel decorated with lemons while shopping? Buy it for her and drop it off at her house with a note.

# Conclusion

*Dancing into the Future*

I AM PROUD OF YOU! THE FACT THAT YOU MADE IT through Take 7 and are taking action on your dreams is *everything*.

Now that you've done all this healing to figure out what it is that you really want, *dream big*. Commit to what you *really* want. If you're just interested in something, you'll lose steam. But if you commit, you'll get there.

Is it going to be easy? No. Committing to your champion self is not easy. (I like to call it interesting.) But you are chosen by God to be here on this earth for such a time as this. You're on your way to reaching your potential. You're about to see the seeds God planted in you come out in a harvest.

Deciding to live life on purpose takes courage. Most people

don't have that. You've made it all the way to the end of this book. You're not like most people. Could you experience more joy? Experience more satisfaction in your relationships? Your spiritual life? Come up with a new business idea that generates additional income?

Imagine using Take 7 on a regular basis. Where could you be in 90 days, 365 days, or 2,000 days from now? Many people overestimate what they can accomplish in a year and underestimate what can happen in five years. The compounding effect happens over time. Your actions add up. As you act with intention, you will be in alignment with God's will for your life and favor will follow you.

Years ago, I decided what I really wanted was great friends in my life who loved me for me and not for what I could do for them. Acting in the direction of that vision involved a move to a new city where I knew no one, but it was near the ocean, which was a part of my dream life. I couldn't imagine meeting the kind of amazing friends that I dreamed of yet didn't really believe truly existed. But that brave move put me in the right environment to meet them.

Once I was in my happy place by the ocean, Little Me felt safe to let my champion self make moves. I took my kids to a playdate at their new school and a few of the other moms there became my buds. Why was I able to meet these wonderful women? Because I got honest about what I really wanted and then acted in the direction of my desires. I want the same thing for you.

I use Take 7 daily. It's the essential tool in my emotional and mental tool kit. You're going to find so many ways to put it to work. Do I answer all the questions every time I get stuck? No.

Sometimes answering just one gets me unstuck and I'm good to go. When I need a deeper dive, I start at question 1 and work through all of them. They work for life change and they work for daily decision making. I use them when I'm interacting with my family. I use them when I get triggered by something. It's simple, but it's not one-and-done like your favorite chocolate chip cookie recipe. Sometimes what worked a year ago won't work now.

I also highly recommend doing a life audit once a quarter. Or do it when the seasons change. Whatever works for you! Plug it into your calendar. When it pops up, go through the Freedom Wheel. Use Take 7 to ask, "What is not working for me in _____?" (health, wealth, etc.).

You can go further and faster than you ever thought possible. Put your hand over your chest. Take a deep breath. Feel your heartbeat. You're alive. You're here, and that means you're here for a purpose. You have the power to create the life you dream of. You can live out your purpose with passion every day. And the riches will follow!

Reading this book won't change your life. But acting on your answers to Take 7 will. One hundred percent. You were created for abundance, meaning, and connection. Now go after your dreams by being the person you're made to be!

# The Take 7 Questions

1. What's Not Working for Me in My Life?
2. When Did I First Start Accepting That?
3. What Little Me Is Showing Up Right Now?
4. What Is a Better Way of Looking at This?
5. Where Is There Space for Gratitude in This?
6. What Do I *Really* Want?
7. What Is the Best Next Step for Me?

# The Best Way to Start and End Your Day

I'M COMMITTED TO SHOWING UP FEELING FABU-lous, head to toe. How else am I going to be fully present—not hanging back, nervous and awkward? I plan to bring the energy up everywhere I go, with gratitude and grace. I can't do any of that if I feel sloppy or messy or worn out. So I take care of myself physically. I work out regularly with a trainer, eat well, and protect my exposure to negativity. I invest in self-care because I know my own worth.

## Start the Day

I fill up before I go out by waking up an hour before anyone else in my house. It's my way of putting *first things first*. Do I check email or social media? No, I head straight to my meeting. See, I have a standing meeting with my CEO: God! I put on my Bose headphones and turn on worship music. (After all, this is *my* time—I'm not waking anyone up!) I pull out my Bible, seeking God's wisdom, searching the Word, and listening to God's leading. I ask the Holy Spirit to reveal which relationships to nurture and which to avoid. And I listen. I listen to his leading and I brain dump any thoughts I have into a journal so that I can have more clarity.

God's opinion matters most to me. Not my best friend's or my mom's. I go to God first. That's been a tough habit to implement, but it has been a game changer.

I want to be the right person at the right place at the right time. I can't do this without staying tuned in to what God has for me. I need his input. He's my rescuer, helper, redeemer, and Creator—he's the ultimate innovator and artist. I bring my goals to him, inviting him into the building of my life, talking through my dreams and plans. I ask him to strip pride out of my goals and to let his purpose infuse them, to bring people alongside me in pursuit of *his* plans.

Have you ever walked out of a meeting so energized, knowing something special has just happened? That's how I feel after my morning meeting. After that I get to work, surrendering the results to God and what he wants. It might all sound woo-woo to you, and that's okay. I know it works. God is coaching me! I have seen such an uptick in productivity and joy. I'm learning to be a better leader and a mom and a wife. He's coaching me to be even more generous as the company grows so that everyone's wealth rises together. I ask God what he wants me to do with the proceeds of our business, and the clarity he provides is amazing. Participating with him builds our relationship, and it assures me of my purpose in his plan.

Even if you're unfamiliar with the Bible, I encourage you to give it a try. There are so many transformative principles there, whether you have made God the CEO of your life or not. Even if you aren't a believer, if you follow kingdom principles, you will be blessed. The fire of God inspires and propels me even on hard days.

People often say to me, "You talk about the Bible all the time. I'm going to have to check it out." I love that. I recommend starting with the book of Proverbs, which has undeniably true words of wisdom. It'll get you hooked. Then read Matthew. That's where you get to meet Jesus and that's where it gets truly, undeniably good. Give it a chance—like any new thing you might try. It might feel awkward at first, but after a while you start to see things in a new light. You start to crave it.

With Scripture saturating my heart and mind, I can go about my day filled with confidence and peace. I rebuke any disturbances of my mindset in Jesus' name. I remember how he said "Peace! Be still!" to the roaring waves and suddenly "there was a great calm" (Mark 4:39). That's not just peace, that's power!

## Prioritize Time

My soul gets fed before my family gets fed. That may not be you. I recently spent time with Kristen Wilkerson. She reminded me that it says nothing in the Bible about us having to have a quiet time in the morning. With a newborn at home, Kristen says she's taking time with God where she can get it.

God wants a relationship with us, and if we're honest, we know we need it more than he does. Spend time where you have the time. If it's a priority for you, you'll make the time. You can do it in the car or waiting in line. But—just being real with you here—maybe check your screen time on your phone. The time you spend on apps might be put to better use. Scrolling for inspiration will give you a hit of pleasure for a minute, but the amount of information we are getting bombarded with on our phones is unreal. Social media throws more at us in five minutes than we need in five days. It messes with our brain chemistry, pumping us full of dopamine (pleasure) and cortisol (stress).

Try swapping out app time with CEO time. Maybe you can decide not to check your phone first thing—that can be CEO time. Or instead of scrolling in the carpool line, put the phone down and open the Word. It might take some resolve or discipline, but you will see results so quickly. And once you do, you will find you never want to miss your morning meeting with your CEO.

Think about the time you spend in your car. What are you consuming during that time? I get to drive my eight-year-old and my ten-year-old to school. On that drive, sometimes I imagine I'm delivering them to the lions' den and I need to prepare them for that. There is so much that can go wrong at school. It's important that they're equipped with critical thinking and how to be a powerful human being. So we have great conversations on that drive.

I declare Scripture over all our lives. We speak powerful Scripture aloud. Thinking about the helmet of salvation really renews our mind to think positively about the day ahead. We pick a Scripture of the day. I ask them, "What's your plan for going out of your way to be kind—to be the change you want to see in the world? To be light bearers?" We're developing the habit of connecting with God through his Word before stepping into the larger world. If it's important for me to do it as an adult, how much more equipping is it for a child who's still in formation? I want it for myself as an adult, so I want it for my children just as much.

## End the Day

How are you ending your day? The rule at my house is no screens an hour before bed. It's way too easy to scroll to sleep. That is not a recipe for good dreams. That's why I unplug from media at 8 p.m. and spend screen-free time reading, reflecting, and journaling, preparing for good sleep and powerful dreams. I read faith-building scriptures (I've posted some great ones at caylac-raft.com!). Journaling about my day helps me feel calm and joyful and more clear about who I am. It gives me such a strong sense of supernatural favor and protection.

Prayer is another way I connect with God. When you think about prayer, think about the blessings in your life, pray over your next day, and think about the promises of God that you need to meditate on in this moment. Build a Noah-like faith in this crazy world. Noah heard from God that he was supposed to build this enormous boat when there was no water close by. He was focused on the dreams God had given him. The world thought he was nuts. He built this huge ark, collected all these animals, and brought them on board the boat. He was on mission. Intentional. When you're focused and on mission, sometimes you'll get the Noah treatment. People might laugh. You will be told no. You will be told no a lot. Your plans and dreams will be met with resistance. Let that fortify you. Be a Noah. Have that Noah-like focus.

As you go through Take 7, I pray you'll believe even more of God. I pray you'll see miraculous growth and change. And I pray that you'll feel and embrace the full love of God for every part of who you are and who you're becoming!

# Connecting with Little You

## Exercise 1: Getting to Know Little You

Recall your earliest memory and use the following prompts to help connect with Little You.

- Do you know approximately what age you were? _____
  _____

- Can you remember what you were wearing? _____
  _____

- Where were you? _____
  _____

- What is Little You feeling? _____
  _____

- What does she need to hear from you? _____
  _____

- What would you say to that little version of yourself? _____
  _____

- What would you tell her about herself? _____
  _____

- What's true about her? _____
  _____

- Your inner child is the most innocent, loving, and joyful part of you. I believe that your inner child is pointing you to God's voice inside you—the One who knows what you need and how you need to be loved and nurtured. He knows what those late-night no-one-sees tears are really about and understands the tender parts of you that carry on no matter how old you are.

Spend a few minutes pondering these truths about your inner child:

- Little You is loved.
- She is worthy just because she was born—not because of anything she did or didn't do.
- She is a child of God, who has amazing plans for her life.
- She belongs.
- She is meant for a beautiful life, not for pain or struggle.
- She is *not* alone.
- She doesn't have to do it all by herself.
- She can be safe in joy. She is safe.

## **Exercise 2: Playing with Little You**

What would being playful look like for you? What would the Little You do to be in joy and play today?

_____

_____

_____

Play is healing because it gives that part of you permission to be in joy and delight without having to work or earn it. Whatever being playful is for you, that's how to engage your inner child.

Do something that makes you giggle, want to dance, feel cozy inside—whether it's playing with a favorite childhood toy (one you had or one you always wanted) or simply allowing yourself to _play_. This frees up creative ideas and flow.

# Exercise 3: Writing with Little You

*Caution:* This exercise can be triggering and even lead to dissociation. If you have a history of PTSD symptoms or dissociative reactions, it would be wise to involve a professional therapist or counselor. For everyone, consider having a trusted support person nearby to help ground you during or after the exercise, if needed. Use caution and pay attention to your inner knowing to decide when or if there is a safe time to complete this. For those who can do it, I believe that there is almost no more powerful exercise.[i]

●

*Setup:* Before doing this exercise make sure you're in a safe space physically and feel safe emotionally. Allow plenty of time so there's room to process whatever memories come up. (Example: Don't do this right before an appearance or intensive meeting. Have a cushion of time to recover.)

1. Connect to a deep memory of you as your younger self, one that brings up emotions. See the world from her eyes.
2. With your nondominant hand (if you are right-handed, use your left hand, or vice versa), write a letter from the perspective of Little You. Let it flow cathartically—don't edit, don't judge. It'll likely feel slow, it will be messy, and it will look childlike.
3. Sometimes your writing will initially feel blocked, so if this

---

i. The nondominant hand exercise is courtesy of art therapist Lucia Capacchione.

is your first time, just write whatever comes for as long as it comes. Writing with the nondominant hand accesses regions of the memory and brain that are not easily accessed in our conscious state, so this can be a powerful remover of blocks.[1]

4. When the exercise feels complete, take the pen in your dominant hand and write from your current perspective. Remind Little You what's true about her, who she is, and what her value is. Address as many areas raised from her letter as you can. Avoid suppressing emotions—rather, remind her that it's understandable for her to feel that way because of the circumstances. Then remind her of what's true.

5. Take time to pause, breathe, and congratulate yourself for unearthing deep emotions that were buried in order to stay safe.

# Exercise 4: Celebrating Little You

You become a more wise, more loving, more mature adult when you learn to heal, listen to, love, and be joyful with your inner child. Healing your child self helps you become your best adult self. You are created as a wise and loving person at your core—no matter what any other messages may have told you. Hold gratitude for that truth.

- Write your "superstar" list of ways in which you can see the wisdom and love you have in your life. Write all that you've accomplished, listing everything you can think of (no editing!) as a way of expressing gratitude to yourself and for yourself, knowing God entrusted your soul and your inner child to you purposefully.
- Celebrate the little girl part of you just like you would any other child in your life. Do something to celebrate your gratitude for Little You! Buy yourself flowers or do an activity that is fun and joyful.
- Look at yourself in the mirror. Look into your eyes and speak aloud the words your inner child needs to hear:
  "I love you."
  "I forgive you."
  "I'm proud of you."
  "God is always taking care of you. He delights in *you*."
- Add in some specifics like
  "You did a great job with _____"
  "You are really gifted at_____"

"It's okay to want _____"
"You were made for a purpose, on purpose."

As you nurture yourself, you'll nurture feelings of confidence and self-love that are greatly healing. There's no shame in self-love. When you love God, then love *you*, you can love others.

## Exercise 5: Meet Little You's Needs

**Note:** This exercise can be done in just a few minutes and is designed to be completed numerous times a day as you see the photo and check in with Little You.

1. Identify the version of yourself that is currently "driving the bus" or needs support or healing.
2. Place a photo of yourself *at that age* where you will see it daily.
3. When you see it, be curious, exploring what she needs. With intention, act to *be* who she needs you to be. In other words, be the adult that Little You needed by taking steps toward the life you *really* want.[ii]

---

ii. With thanks to Dr. Jenn Chrisman.

# Acknowledgments

I WANT TO ACKNOWLEDGE MY AMAZING CLIENT Amy VanSlambrook for providing insightful exercises that she's used in her therapy practice. Amy, the world is blessed to have you.

Thank you to my longtime friend Dr. Jenn for also giving exercises and always loving on little Cayla so kindly over the years.

To all my clients who shaped this methodology, I love all of you so much, and watching you get what you really want in life has been my *why*.

# Notes

## CHAPTER 1: WHAT'S YOUR STORY?

1. Michelle McLeary, "Scientists Finally Show How Your Thoughts Can Cause Specific Molecular Changes to Your Genes," Michelle McLeary (website), accessed August 23, 2023, https://michellemcleary.nl/coaching /scientists-finally-show-thoughts-change-genes/.
2. Jennice Vilhauer, "How Your Thinking Affects Your Brain Chemistry," *Psychology Today*, April 10, 2023, https://www.psychologytoday.com/us /blog/living-forward/202304/how-your-thinking-affects-your-brain-chemistry.
3. "Why Our Brains Love Story," UCI Center for the Neurobiology of Learning and Memory, December 4, 2018, https://cnlm.uci.edu/2018/12/04/story.

## CHAPTER 2: LITTLE YOU

1. Shirley Davis, "The Wounded Inner Child," CPTSD Foundation, July 13, 2020, https://cptsdfoundation.org/2020/07/13/the-wounded-inner-child.
2. Alex Miguel Meyer, "Subconscious Mind & Inner Child Explained: The Key to Wellbeing," Medium, June 20, 2020, https://medium.com/invisible-illness /the-subconscious-mind-inner-child-explained-511b1ef93c7f.
3. Jeffrey L. Fannin and Robert M. Williams, "What Neuroscience Reveals About the Nature of Business" (paper, 2011), https://www.academia.edu /66291763/What_Neuroscience_Reveals_about_the_Nature_of_Business.

## CHAPTER 3: YOU ARE YOUR BIGGEST ASSET

1. Jolene Brighten, *Is This Normal? Judgment-Free Straight Talk About Your Body* (New York: Simon & Schuster, 2023).

## CHAPTER 4: FROM LIMITING BELIEFS TO UNLIMITED POTENTIAL

1. Scott Mautz, "A Harvard Psychologist Shows How to Change Those Limiting Beliefs You Still Have About Yourself," *Inc.*, accessed August 23, 2023, https://www.inc.com/scott-mautz/a-harvard-psychologist-shows-how-to-change-those-limiting-beliefs-you-still-have-about-yourself.html.
2. Colleen Vanderlinden, "It's True—You Really Should Talk to Your Plants," The Spruce, updated February 17, 2022, https://www.thespruce.com/should-you-talk-to-your-plants-3972298.
3. For more inspiration, visit https://caylacraft.com/walk.

## CHAPTER 5: VOICE IT

1. Eva M. Krockow, "How Many Decisions Do We Make Each Day?," *Psychology Today*, September 27, 2018, https://www.psychologytoday.com/us/blog/stretching-theory/201809/how-many-decisions-do-we-make-each-day.

## CHAPTER 8: REFRAME IT

1. "Spark Creativity by Changing Location," *Inc.*, January 31, 2019, https://www.inc.com/ford-transit-connect/tip-of-the-day/spark-creativity-by-changing-location.html.
2. *Crafted Entrepreneur*, https://caylacraft.com/podcast.

## CHAPTER 10: DEEP DESIRE

1. Check out some vision prayers at caylacraft.com.

## CHAPTER 11: ACT NOW

1. Chris Horymski, "Credit Scores Steady as Consumer Debt Balances Rise in 2022," Experian, February 24, 2023, https://www.experian.com/blogs/ask-experian/consumer-credit-review/#s4.

## CONNECTING WITH LITTLE YOU

1. Lucia Capacchione, *The Power of Your Other Hand: Unlock Creativity and Inner Wisdom Through the Right Side of Your Brain* (Newburyport, MA: Red Wheel, 2019).

# About the Author

CAYLA CRAFT IS A DYNAMIC EMPOWERMENT CAT-
alyst, business strategist, and inspirational speaker known for
her unwavering commitment to helping individuals transform
their lives and achieve their fullest potential. With a charismatic
presence and a passionate mission, Cayla has inspired countless
individuals around the world to break free from limitations,
embrace their unique strengths, and create the life of their dreams.

Her journey to becoming a leading voice in personal development and empowerment was shaped by her own life experiences.
Born and raised in sunny California, Cayla navigated through
challenging circumstances and setbacks that compelled her to
seek a higher purpose. Her resilience, determination, and unwavering belief in the power of personal growth became the driving
force behind her transformational journey.

A dynamic personality, authentic approach, transformative
insights, and natural ability to connect with people have made

ABOUT THE AUTHOR

Cayla a sought-after coach and mentor. She has dedicated her life to uplifting individuals and guiding them on their path to success. As the founder of Mommy Millionaire and Crafted Entrepreneur, Cayla is particularly committed to helping women shatter glass ceilings, break free from limiting beliefs, and achieve financial independence.

At the heart of Cayla's mission is the belief that we all have the power to rewrite our stories and create extraordinary lives. Her dedication to helping others discover their inner strength and pursue their passions has made her a beacon of inspiration in the personal development and empowerment community.

Explore her latest book to embark on your own journey of personal growth and empowerment.